Searching for the New Normal

Tom + Melodi,
    I am so very glad our paths crossed a few years ago. you are both very dear and special to me + Karl. I am very proud and honored to call you friend. I truly give thanks for friends such as yourselves. Take care and I hope our paths cross again, face to face in the very near future.

Love,
Leſanne
Williams

Searching for the New Normal

❖

My personal journal as my greatest fear is
realized—the death of my child.

Rexanne Williams

iUniverse, Inc.
New York Lincoln Shanghai

Searching for the New Normal
My personal journal as my greatest fear is realized—the death of my child.

iUniverse books may be ordered through booksellers or by contacting:

iUniverse
2021 Pine Lake Road, Suite 100
Lincoln, NE 68512
www.iuniverse.com
1-800-Authors (1-800-288-4677)

Because of the dynamic nature of the Internet, any Web addresses or links contained in this book may have changed since publication and may no longer be valid.

The views expressed in this work are solely those of the author and do not necessarily reflect the views of the publisher, and the publisher hereby disclaims any responsibility for them.

Cover concept and design by Reed Hill, reed-hill.com

ISBN: 978-0-595-45242-2 (pbk)
ISBN: 978-0-595-71374-5 (cloth)
ISBN: 978-0-595-89553-3 (ebk)

Printed in the United States of America

Contents

Acknowledgements

I want to give my heartfelt thanks to my therapist, Jodie Moore, because this book would have forever remained my personal journal if it had not been for her inspiring words of wisdom and kindness. She strongly encouraged me to put my journal in print to help the many others who are now feeling what I felt those first three years. It was her words of encouragement that have now brought this book to you. We often hear that there are angels amongst us. She will gladly tell you that she is a mere therapist but when I talk about her I tell everyone that she is my angel who rescued an extremely wounded soul. I know God put her in my path to help me deal with something that I would have never been able to do on my own. When I get to heaven I look forward to the day that I can introduce her to my son Daniel. It will be nice to finally have her meet him because she certainly knows everything there is to know about Daniel.

I am very thankful to my editor and good friend Jerry Billings who not only spent many hours on my book but was also my bishop at the time of Daniel's death. His love and comfort was extended at a very critical time in my life and was well received by me and my family.

I have never doubted that there have been people that were placed in my path when I needed them. They have made this journey so much sweeter than I could have ever imagined. I have met the nicest and kindest people in my quest of publishing this journal. Thank you Molly O'Bryan at iUniverse for always being there to answer my many questions and making me feel as though I were your number one priority each and every time I called.

I have so much appreciation and gratitude for my new friend, Paul Reed. Paul designed the amazing book cover. He is a principle of Reed-Hill (www.reed-hill.com), in Castle Rock, Colorado. Paul came into my life at the critical point when it was time to choose the book cover design. Not only did I not know what Paul's occupation was, I had never met Paul until it was time to design the cover. It still amazes me to see the people that have come into my life right at the moment that I needed them the most. Thank you so much Paul and thank you for having such strong emotional feelings towards the book which gave you the drive for this incredible cover.

Foreword

"There is nothing as devastating as the loss of a child." This statement is spoken by bereaved parents of every walk of life. All other suffering will pale in comparison to the pain of losing a beloved son or daughter. This pain is complicated, exacerbated, and magnified when the child intentionally brings about his or her own demise.

The journey to reconciliation to this loss is arduous and long for most loved ones. Many travel it alone because of fear of stigma or because of others' inability to relate. This can be a hard journey requiring strength and perseverance at a time when both are in short supply. Often, loved ones desperately need another person to companion them on their journey, to share the experience and perhaps provide a sense of universality-that none of us is alone in the search of understanding and healing in the aftermath of staggering loss.

Rexanne Williams is such a person. She invites us along on her own very personal and searing journey through the wilderness of her grief after the completed suicide of her nineteen year old son, Daniel. And though this recounting is a deeply personal exploration of the death of her son by suicide, it is also a moving and illuminating study of a family in crisis who moves from brokenness to wholeness through the power of relationship. It is also a testimony to the enduring power of love that transcends even the grave.

Come join Rexanne on her journey, meet Daniel and his family, explore the indomitable power of the human spirit, and search the heart of the Divine in the context of this most wrenching of experiences. You may find yourself in these pages, and discover your own peace.

Come journey with us …

Joanne (Jodie) Moore, LPC, NCC, BCETS, … Stillwaters Counseling, Virginia Beach, VA

Introduction

This book is written for anyone experiencing grief especially a mother or father who has lost a child. On March 2, 2003, my nineteen year old son Daniel took his own life. The manner in which your child has died may be the only difference you and I share. The grief we now feel after the death of our dear cherished children puts us in a very distinct group of people. Parents are not supposed to bury their children. This isn't normal nor is it the cycle of life.

I knew how desperately I wanted to read another mother's story and I could not find it so now I give you my story. This book does not contain any therapeutic thoughts dealing with grief or in depth studies of suicide. This book can easily be described as raw grief. No rose colored glasses were worn to give any other description other than what was taken directly from the pages of my journal. The pages of this book deal with the very raw and painful side of grief because it is the true and actual account of my experience in dealing with grief.

This book that you are now holding in your hands was never intended to be a book. I began my journal seven days after my son took his own life. This journal became a great place for me to unleash waves and waves of emotions such as pain, grief, anger, and a sadness that was indescribable. I never knew it was humanly possible to feel so much pain and sadness and yet have the human body still survive.

There were so many days that I was sure that I was going crazy. I felt sure that I was losing my mind and I was the only mother who had such feelings because of the death of a child. I would have given anything if I had been able to pick up a book and read for myself that another parent had experienced the same feelings I was then experiencing. I was searching desperately for information that would let me confirm that I was not the only one who had had those feelings and emotions. And most importantly, I would have discovered that as horrible and devastating those feelings were I was not going crazy and I was going to survive.

The journal was divided into chapters. The chapter titles and subtitles were added for publication and for the ease of reading.

A Mother's Note

I started this personal journal seven days after my son took his own life. You will read the first names of my other children. It is with their permission that I have used their real names. Please note that this is my personal journal and not a family journal. For those who may be concerned or curious I would like all to know that our entire family did go into counseling immediately to help us deal with this tragic loss. I will not be giving any information on intimate details on how the children did in the following weeks and months following Daniel's death. That is their personal and private information. This book is my story, the journal of a mother who lost her son to suicide.

My children's names are mentioned in this journal many times and for this reason I feel it is important that I introduce them to you in hopes that it will make the reading of this book easier to follow.

At the time of Daniel's death Laurie, my oldest, was twenty-seven. She is married to Mike, has three children and lives in the area. Joseph, my oldest son was twenty-five and was at the University of Florida. Melissa is my third child and was twenty-four. She is married to Tim and they had one child and they also live in the area. Michael is child number four and was twenty-two years old and was living in Provo, Utah. Daniel is child number five. Jennifer is child number six and was sixteen years old. Amy is child number seven and was fourteen years old. Matthew is number eight and was eleven years old.

Chapter 1

That Day

"The first day of the rest of my life"

March 9, 2003
"… I had thoughts of gratitude that I had never lost a child …"

I am not sure how you ever first put pen to paper in the pages of a journal that you know you are keeping for the thoughts you have about the death of your son. One week ago today I lost my Daniel, my baby boy who was nineteen years old. Do I first write every thought I have of Daniel and tell whoever may read this journal that Daniel was the core of his mother's heart? Or do I start by re-living all the events of last Sunday? Perhaps I'll begin with last Sunday only because it is so fresh in my mind and I relive it everyday sometimes as often as every hour.

I awoke last Sunday morning at 8:10. At first I was startled to see the clock because I had overslept. Karl, my husband, had been ill during the night and was still sleeping. I always get up an hour earlier on Sundays because Karl leaves for an early church meeting. I quickly got up and asked Karl if he was going to church. He said, "yes, but I am going in later because I was sick during the night and I have overslept." I went to Matt's, Amy's and Jenny's bedrooms to tell them I had overslept and to hurry and get up. I came downstairs to tell Daniel to get up. I opened his door and called his name. Daniel's bedroom was the room over the garage and you have to go up 10 or 12 steps to enter his room. I called from the bottom of the stairs. I called his name just a couple of times and asked if he were going to church? He answered, "I don't know." Those were the last words that Daniel would ever speak to me.

I told Daniel it was 8:10 and we had all overslept. We all needed to hurry and get to church because church started at 9:00 and we were running late. I turned and left. Oh, I wish I had gone up those stairs. I wish I had seen him when I spoke to him. Would I have been able to see any signs? Would I have been able to see anything that was out of the norm? Would I have been able to tell that he was upset or sad? I would give anything to live that morning over again. I want so desperately to believe that I would have seen or detected something. I would have never left him and we would have sat on his bed and talked and talked until I knew his crisis was over. I don't care how long it would have taken as long as I knew I was sitting with him.

Amy had been ill the entire week before with the flu and had not been able to go to school. As I saw she wasn't moving very quickly I opted to let her sleep in. I'd give her another day to rest and prepare to go back to school tomorrow. Matt wasn't moving very fast either so I decided to let him come later with Karl simply because we were in a hurry and running late. Jenny and I made it to church on time. In the chapel I chose a pew nearly at the front on the right side. No matter what city we have lived in or what church building we attend we always sit in the same pew in the same location. It's the middle section of pews and fourth row from the back. Jenny questioned my choice on that Sunday and I had no answer as to why. It just felt like everything about that morning was strange and different. Karl did make it to church about an hour and half later and church continued as usual. I taught the women's Relief Society lesson that morning. I taught the history of Emma Smith in honor of the anniversary month of Relief Society. As I stood and taught I realized a few similarities between Emma's life and mine. I too had once had a baby without a husband being home. When Michael was born Karl was deployed on a ship in the Navy. Karl had been deployed so many times in the Navy and I too had had countless sleepless nights. I had nights with so much loneliness for my husband that I never knew how I was going to make it. Yes, there were a couple of things that I easily related to when studying the life of Emma but I always knew there was one huge difference between us. She had endured one of life's greatest tests. She had to suffer the loss of a child. I felt for her because of her losses but I had not known until that day what she had truly experienced. As I taught the lesson I had thoughts of gratitude that I had never lost a child and that I had been spared that trial.

Jenny and I got home from church about 12:40 P.M. Karl soon followed us in. Jenny and I became very busy getting ready for Sunday dinner. The first Sunday of each month all the children, spouses and grandchildren come over for dinner. Daniel's door was shut and I heard music so I quickly knew where he was. Amy was still in her room and Matt and Karl were changing their clothes. It was shortly after one o'clock when Tim, Missy and Emily came in. We were all excited to hear about their first Sunday in their new ward at church. They had moved the week before and this was their first Sunday. They were excited to tell us how welcomed they felt and the immediate friends they felt they had made. We were all in the kitchen and anxious for Laurie, Mike and their children to arrive. We were all so hungry. The final touches were being put on the table and I knew Laurie would be walking in any minute. In fact we were so close to sitting down that I had asked Matt to come and fix his plate. He usually ate in the kitchen with the younger grandchildren due to the lack of room at the dining room table. I had also asked Karl to please tell Daniel it was time to eat.

Now isn't it strange that the pen has flowed so easily till this very moment on the page when I write, "go tell Daniel to come and eat." Because you see it's at this very moment that you realize our lives will never ever be the same again. Perhaps if I don't write it in print then it's not true. I also know if I write it then it must not be a nightmare, but unfortunately it's true.

Karl went to Daniel's door and discovered that it was locked. Daniel's door is never locked. Never. Maybe once or twice when he locked it when he was going somewhere and he didn't want the little kids in his room while he was gone. I was standing beside Matt at the dining room table and my heart felt like it skipped a beat. I knew then something was not right because he had locked his door. I heard Karl banging on the door and calling his name over and over with no response. Karl asked if we had a key to that door and I felt sure we did. We met each other in the home office and I found several key rings with a couple of keys on them. I gave all of them to Karl and told him I felt sure that Daniel's door key was on one of those rings. I went back in the dining room to assist Matt. I could hear Karl trying to find the right key. I remember feeling relieved when I heard the door open thinking oh good there was the right key on one of those rings. At this precise moment I can see myself standing right beside Matt at the dining room table. I then heard the **MOST** horrific, unbelievable screaming coming from Karl. Karl was yelling Daniel's name over and over. I took off running so fast that I literally kicked off my shoes in the kitchen hoping to even run faster. I know that because I have visions of me later in the day walking around in my bare feet. And much later, hours later my shoes were found on the little mat in front of the kitchen sink. I remember thinking how strange my shoes look. Someone has completely come in and cleaned up my kitchen and my shoes are just sitting here in front of the sink. They looked so out of place. So as I ran out of my shoes towards Daniel's room I began to climb the steps. Karl realized it was me coming into the room and he began yelling for me not to come any further. "Do not come in but go get Tim," was what he was yelling. But it was too late I had already seen the most unbelievable sight in the world. Karl's overprotection and love for me could not protect me from what I saw. I had only come up a few stairs so I had a limited view. I could tell Karl was trying to hold Daniel up as he had grabbed Daniel from the back around his waist. I saw Karl's back but I also saw it. I saw the leather belt hanging from the light fixture and could see it attached to Daniel's neck. I wasn't able to see his face because Daniel's head was drooping down. I screamed and ran down the stairs yelling for Tim. I remember Tim running up the stairs and passing me. Tim began to scream, "oh my God, oh my God, no, no, no!" Missy came up only a few steps when Tim yelled to her to call 911. I was still screaming! Now all this is happening in a matter of seconds but it feels like everything is in real slow motion and this is taking minutes and minutes. Missy took off running down the steps. I went down into the kitchen for what felt like minutes but I know it was only a matter of seconds. I started back up the stairs and once again Karl asked that I not come upstairs. I was able to peer in and I could see that Daniel was now lying on the floor. I saw Daniel's legs and could see his feet and legs looked almost black. I then followed up his body and saw Karl and Tim kneeling over the top of Daniel. I saw his head but mostly his left side of his cheek. It was so blue or gray in color. I remember asking Karl if he was dead. Karl yelled back, "yes." That was all he said and he said it with such force and loudness. It felt like that one little word resonated in my soul and touched the deepest parts of my soul. I can remember screaming and screaming over and over, "NO, NO, NO not Daniel!" It was if I had no control. I can actually remember going into the home office and seeing Missy on the phone. I knew she had called 911. I kept thinking they wouldn't be able to hear her and she can't hear them so I must hush. But I couldn't. It was these awful, awful almost primal screams coming from my body and I had no control in stopping. I remember at one point falling to my knees and holding on to the front of the desk in the home office. I have no idea how long I was there. I remember looking up and seeing Laurie drive up out front. I was sad because now she would know.

If she didn't come inside then she wouldn't know. I remember being sad because she was driving which meant she and Mike would be in separate cars. I saw her getting out of her car. I wanted to go to her but I couldn't move. It was as if my legs were bent at the knees and frozen. I could not move but I kept thinking I have to get to Laurie because Mike hasn't gotten here in his truck yet. I have no idea who told that child. I remember her coming in beside me with her little daughter Emma on her hip. She came to me and kept rubbing my shoulder telling me how sorry she was. It felt as though my body weighed 1000's of pounds. I couldn't come to a standing position to hold her and that's all I wanted to do. I remember sobbing and feeling the worst pain I have ever felt in my life. At one point I remember and can see Karl standing beside me on my left. He is rubbing my head and telling me it's going to be all right. My lover, my best friend, and my eternal protector who has just seen the most horrific sight in his life is trying to tell me it is going to be all right. I then realized he has come from Daniel's room. It is also at this point that I begin to hear all these sirens. I can hear Missy telling the 911 dispatcher that they are here now and she hangs up. I remember Karl walking away and I knew I had to get to him. I used all the strength that I could possibly find and forced myself to rise up. I found some kind of inner strength that I didn't know I was capable of. I just knew I had to get to Karl. As I turned around in the office I saw all these police officers coming in the front door. I think it was Tim telling them which way to go. I found Karl in the family room racked with such pain and grief and shock. I have never in my 29 years of knowing Karl have ever seen him in such horrible, unbelievable shape. I remember seeing Mike and being so glad he was now here for Laurie. The police officer asked if there were a pastor or minister or clergy we could call. Someone in the room said a bishop. I got up and went in the home office to get the bishop's phone number and Tim called. I can remember thinking I need to call someone then immediately thinking of Joe and Michael and my mom. I have zero-none-recollection of seeing Amy, Jenny or Matt. I have no idea where they are. I remember an officer asking if I needed the rescue people to offer me medical assistance. I said, "No" and then he asked about Karl and I didn't know how to answer. I went to him and he quickly said, "No."

There seemed to be so much going on. There were lots of law enforcement coming and going. I can remember one time standing in the front foyer by the front door and seeing a very beautiful young female police officer heading towards the door. She had a camera hanging around her neck. I remember thinking she is going to Daniel's room to take Daniel's picture. This beautiful girl is going to take a picture of my son who is dead. I thought what a terrible job to have.

I have snatches of memories that help me remember what was going on. I remember seeing the bishop and he was the first one to arrive outside of the law enforcement. I remember for the first time seeing Amy sitting in the black chair in the office. This is my first memory of seeing her since I left for church early in the morning. I remember going to her and asking if she were all right. I also went to Matt, Jenny, Missy and Laurie and asked if they were ok. Laurie had taken my phone book and had started calling people. I have no idea how that child did it. Where did she possibly find the strength and courage to call her two brothers and two grandmothers? She had also called my best friend and she was on her way. I was in no shape to call anyone much less be able to even think about who needed to be called. I had such an unbelievable sadness for Joe and Michael. They were given the news of their brother's death over the phone and they were so far away. Joe was in Gainesville, FL and Michael was in Provo, Utah. I wanted them home with me to make sure they were ok.

Karl and Tim were both questioned separately by the detectives to get the full and complete details of everything that they could remember. The police seemed to take a long time in Daniel's room. I remember one time walking in the family room and seeing Karl curled up in an almost fetal position on the floor over by the back door. There were such moans and groans coming from him that they almost didn't sound human. I saw Mike, Laurie's husband, quickly go to him and kneel down beside him. He took his father-in-law in his arms and cradled him in his arms and rocked him as if he were a baby. He so lovingly stroked his head and was offering the tenderest loving feelings of comfort and love. I will never forget that picture that is eternally etched in my mind that showed me the true meaning of love and devotion. I hope that I never see Karl in that much pain ever again in his life. It was such unbelievable sadness, utter despair. It was the rawest form of grief that I have ever experienced in my life.

It was soon after that the detective asked that we gather the children and go out on the deck. The men from the medical examiner's office were here to take Daniel's body out of the house and he knew it best if we didn't see this. It is at this point that I realize that the grandchildren are not even here at my house. The in-laws of Laurie and Missy have come and taken the children. I never knew where they were. We go and stand on the deck and the detective pulls the shade that is on the back door. We just stand there and look at each other. This is so unreal and not even imaginable. It is now that I start to cry again. I realize Daniel is leaving this house for the last time and will never return. I also realize that he is going out of his house in a zipped up black body bag. I have always felt some sadness when my older children have left home to go to college, go on missions, and get married. It is such a huge step in their advancing toward adulthood and leaving childhood behind. But this is horrible and no words can adequately describe what I am feeling at that moment. My child is leaving our house for the very last time and he will never return because he has left in a black body bag. Men who never knew my son and don't care about him will take his body out. I'm sure they don't get paid much and this is just a job to them to go and pick up dead bodies. Yet this is my child, a son that will never be replaced and a son that will be loved for eternity.

Daniel's body leaves the house and we are told it's all right to come back inside. The house seems to be buzzing with people who have gotten the word and coming with words of concern and love. I can close my eyes and tell you every person that came that day and night. I can tell you it's not important what you say but it is important that you get to your family and friends when a loss has occurred. The simple hug and whisper in the ear, "I am so sorry" is more than adequate. The stay should be short but let the family know you have heard the news and you care. So many people came through the house that day.

Karl and I were given a gift that afternoon a few short hours after we found Daniel. I know it was a gift. It had to have been because there was so much commotion going on inside the house. There is no possible way that Karl and I could have planned this or even attempted to make this happen. It was much later in the afternoon when I walked through the kitchen and saw Karl standing by himself with his back up against the kitchen sink. I walked up to him and embraced him. We held each other tightly and neither of us wanted to let the other go. This was the first time we had been together by ourselves since Karl had found Daniel. I remember loving the feel of his strength as he held me tight. I backed away from him so I could look directly into his eyes. I took my index finger of my right hand and jabbed it into his chest. As I pointed into his chest and starred into his eyes, I said, "you promise me now, right now that this will not destroy us. We will make it and love each other even more." He looked me directly in the eyes and said, "I promise." From that moment on we had a mission statement with a direct purpose. We had a purpose to go on and keep this family together. I know it was a gift. There is no doubt in my mind. Whether it was from God or Daniel I don't know but it was a gift that on that first day Karl and I could find ourselves standing alone in the kitchen. We were able to make that solemn promise and oath to each other when there was so much more going on in the rest of the house and so many people in the house. There is no doubt it was a gift.

Joe got in Sunday night around 9:00. I was so happy to see him and have him home. A few more people stopped by after 9 and shortly after ten o'clock all went home but the family. We all sat with Joe and filled him in on the details as best we could. Laurie, Mike, Missy and Tim left to go home around 11:00 pm. Karl and I realized we had not eaten one bite all day but neither of us had any desire to eat anything. Karl and I talked to Joe for about another hour. We decided we would attempt to go to bed and see if we could get some needed rest. I went and changed into my gown. Karl and I said our prayers together and I climbed into the bed. I turned off the light beside my bed and closed my eyes. It was immediately that I turned the light back on and sat up. I told Karl I couldn't do it. I can't go to sleep. It was such a fear that paralyzed me. It was as if I knew that if I went to sleep I would have to wake and go through the realization all over again that Daniel was dead. This way if I stayed awake I already knew he was dead and it wouldn't have to hit me again. I came downstairs to find Joe watching TV. We talked for a short time but I knew he was so sleepy and he was fighting it so hard. He was trying so hard to stay awake for me to keep me company. I thought how miserable he looks so I told him I was going to look up something on the Internet in the home office. I was sure he would fall right to sleep if I ever left the room. I spent the rest of the night on the Internet looking at so many web sites about suicide.

I was shocked that over 30,000 suicides occur in the United States each year. There is a suicide every 17 minutes in the United States. More people die of suicide than homicide. It was amazing to me how many white males' ages 15-30 die from suicide. Boys are more successful in their attempts than girls. I thought to myself whatever Daniel did with his body he did a great job. He was so physical and such a gifted athlete. Whatever he did with his body he did extremely well, including killing himself. Why couldn't you have failed at that first attempt? I was surprised to see the room I was sitting in get light with the sun coming in the windows. I had no idea I had spent that many hours at the computer screen reading about suicide. I know my body must have been tired but there was no way I was going to go and lie down. Karl soon got up and found me in the office. I shared with him all the statistics I had learned about suicide during the night. He too was shocked and sad. Too many, far too many! I realize it's no longer March 2. This will be the first day of the rest of my life without Daniel.

Chapter 2

The Funeral

"Death is not the end"

<u>March 12, 2003</u>
"Mom that's not me"

Monday morning, March 3rd began with the stark reality that a funeral needed to be planned. There is not a parent alive that has not felt for another parent when you've heard about the death of a child. You can feel for them because you can only imagine how it would feel to lose a child but that is all it is, mere speculation. Now on top of dealing with the death of Daniel, Karl and I are tasked to go and make funeral arrangements. Sure, there would have been a number of friends and family members who would have easily stepped in and taken over the job but this is something that we both felt had to be done by us. Missy, Laurie and a dear friend went with us. This was very important to have people with us in helping make decisions. It hasn't even been 24 hours and we are now tasked to make big financial decisions. Your mind is cluttered with shock, grief and utter numbness and trying to make even the simplest decisions seem impossible. You are sitting there in this room around a table full of books that offer you choices. People are talking and I know it is important that I pay attention but try as I may I cannot stay focused, I am constantly bringing myself back to try and listen to the conversation of the people in the room. Sometime later we leave with what is a planned funeral. I remember being very attentive when we gave the information for the obituary and when we selected the flowers that would be displayed on top of the casket. Any other details I wouldn't be able to give you.

The house begins to be full of flowers and food. There is so much food and nothing seems to interest me at all. I have no idea who brought the orange juice but I drink several glasses. This feels so good going down and I guess the sugar keeps me going because this is the only thing that I am able to think about putting in my mouth. I am just so grateful that each time I go the refrigerator that there is still orange juice. I take a very special interest in Karl and try on several attempts to get him to eat. I made him several plates of different choices those first few days and he also wants nothing. Karl's time and energy is completely focused on looking at pictures we have of Daniel. After we left the funeral home Karl decided he wanted to do a PowerPoint presentation of Daniel at the viewing. We gathered all our pictures that we could find of Daniel and Karl began to scan them onto the computer. I was grateful for the diversion this would give Karl. I knew he had to get that horrible image of Daniel being dead out of his head. What better way than put hundred's of sweet and cute pictures of Daniel in front of him all day long?

Michael, my mom and Karl's mom all flew in Monday night. I was worried about my mom making the trip by herself and I was very pleased that she had done so well. Words will never be able to express the gratitude I had for a very dear friend who flew home with Michael from Salt Lake City. I knew Michael was taking this extremely hard and I was so worried about him flying by himself. Michael and Daniel were close in age and were very close as brothers growing up together. I knew this would be an extremely difficult time for Michael.

On Tuesday Karl and I went to pick the actual cemetery plot for Daniel to be buried. I knew the cemetery I wanted. It was a nice place but it was not close to the house. I didn't want to be concerned about driving by the cemetery on my daily errands and the very familiar paths I travel on a daily and weekly basis. This would be in a location that I don't travel often and I felt if I visited there it was because I had planned the visit. I never wanted to feel the need to stop just because I was driving by and it would have been hard for me to drive by and not stop. A very dear friend and her husband owned this cemetery. There was comfort in knowing her on such a personal level. Yes, she is a good friend but I never wanted to do business with her. This task seemed so much harder and difficult than the task of preparing for the viewing and funeral. First of all she took us around to several sites and nothing felt right. It has been raining for several days and the ground is soaked and very muddy. I am almost to the point that it doesn't matter. Just tell me where we can put my son's body. I just want this part over. Then she takes us to another section and I immediately know this is right. He would be next to the "baby land" section of the cemetery and right in front of him is the marker of a twelve—year old boy that we were told had died in an automobile accident. If anybody ever looked after the little guys it was Daniel. This is the spot for Daniel, the overseer of the little people. You would think that selecting the burial plot would be the hard part but then we had to go back to the office and do mounds of paper work. You just want to go home and leave this gloomy and sad office. All around you are displays of grave markers. I understand the reason why they give you examples to look at before you purchase but, who is ever in the mood to buy a grave marker? Is there ever a better day than another to buy a grave marker? Now add all that to the realization that you are purchasing a marker for your child's grave. I was glad when it was finally over and that last piece of paper was finally signed. Each time Karl and I left the house and came back we were so amazed at the amount of food and flowers that had been delivered to the house in the amount of time we were gone. When we returned from the cemetery Joe and Karl took Daniel's clothes that had been washed and ironed by a dear friend to the funeral home. It was so easy to pick out what we wanted him buried in. We knew it could only be one outfit, his khaki dress pants, white dress shirt and his yellow tie. He was so good looking and whenever he wore this outfit to church he would cause the girls heads to turn and his mom's heart to swell with such pride. He was so beautiful to look at and he never truly knew how gorgeous he was.

Friends, family, food and flowers continued to pour in. Time seemed to be moving quickly because there were always people to greet and visit when we were home. Karl continued on the PowerPoint presentation and was quite pleased at how well it was turning out. He was almost finished. When we got up Wednesday morning the PowerPoint presentation was no longer on the computer. It was gone. It had totally disappeared from the files of the computer. He was devastated. He had spent hours and hours and now it was all gone. He called in the experts to see if there was anyway to retrieve the missing file. It was a hard dose of reality when he realized he had to start over. The viewing was at 7:00 that night and he wanted the presentation to be ready then. He wanted so badly for there to be pictures of Daniel living for people to see and not to have to focus on Daniel who would be lying in a casket. Daniel was so much more than the deceased

Daniel. Daniel was everything there is about life. As Karl began the tedious task of scanning all the pictures again he called me into the office. He wanted me to know that this was an answer to a prayer. Of course I am quite confused. He tells me that he had been praying and praying that he would find things to stay busy. He didn't want any idle time. He didn't want any time that would allow him to think. He wanted to stay constantly busy so he wouldn't have to think. He realized the night before that he was almost finished and he wondered what he could possibly do now to stay busy. Having to re-do the PowerPoint was a definite distraction and something that would fill his time very easily. So he began the time consuming task of scanning all those pictures of Daniel again. He was able to complete the second copy of Daniel's slide presentation in time to take it to the viewing. It was so good and so many people commented on how much they enjoyed seeing it. It was certainly made with lots and lots of love and tireless devotion by Daniel's father.

In making the funeral arrangements we had agreed on two viewings. The first would be Wednesday afternoon for immediate family members. The second viewing would be Wednesday evening. We had agreed that I, Karl, the children, their spouses, the two grandmothers and my brother would come to the first viewing. I had known that this would be the most difficult part of the entire week. I don't know why but I remember a long time ago someone asked what they thought would be the most horrible thing to happen to me. The answer came immediately and still remains. The hardest thing that would ever be asked of me would be to see one of my children in a casket. The family viewing was planned for 3:00 in the afternoon. As we are driving over to the funeral home I am sitting in the back seat. I am saying over and over again to myself, "Daniel you have got to help me. This is going to be the hardest part and I can't do this by myself. You have got to help me get through this." We entered the front door of the funeral home and Karl and I were the first to enter and we were holding hands. The others were following closely behind us. The director walked us down a hall and then he opened two large size French doors. Immediately in front of us I can see Daniel lying in the casket. I don't realize it but Karl has let go of my hand and has dropped back in the hallway. The children tell me later that he became very emotional and could not enter the room. I had a totally different reaction. I saw my baby and was drawn to him. It was almost as if I couldn't get to him fast enough. I immediately found myself standing directly beside him at the casket. The most devastating feelings of pain and sadness came over me as I looked upon the face of that still beautiful human being. My crying was more like long mournful sobs. As I stood there by myself I hear the most audible voice. It was so clear and distinct that I turned to the left because I was sure that I would see him standing right next to me. The voice was there but no body. He said, "Mom, that's not me. That's not me in that box. I am not there." I immediately felt such peace and comfort. It was such a feeling that I will never be able to adequately describe as long as I live. It's impossible to describe something that is indescribable. I know with every fiber of my being it was Daniel and yet I have no earthly idea how he did it. I know it was him because of the sound of his voice and what he said. That would have definitely been my Daniel to say that's not me in the box. Daniel would have definitely used the word box and not said casket. This enormous amount of peace and comfort swept all through me. I was instantly available to go to Karl and the rest of the family and offer them peace, comfort and strength. Daniel had indeed done what I had so recently asked. He helped his mother view him in the casket. It was a far greater thing than I could ever had imagined or ever dreamt to ask. The spirit does indeed go on and death is not the end. I had definitely been visited by my Daniel's spirit and I knew he was very aware of my earthly existence.

As I was able to go to each individual child I realized that they too were feeling the Comforter. It was a physical presence and yet there is no way to express in words something that cannot be seen or heard. I knew and we all knew that God had not left us to deal this with horrific tragedy by ourselves. The children became quite concerned that Daniel's hair did not look right. The staff at the funeral home had parted his hair in the middle. Never would Daniel have gone out in public with his hair parted in the middle and the children knew it. Daniel was not conceited but he definitely took a great interest in how he looked. There is a large mirror in the downstairs foyer by the front door. Daniel always took one last look in that mirror to make sure every hair was in place and he looked his best before leaving the house. The staff had overheard concerns about his hair and said they always do the best they can but never seeing the person before makes it hard to know how to do their hair. He told us that they had a comb and hairspray if we would like to use it. The children eagerly agreed to try it. With only a few attempts it was realized they needed Daniel's Mega Hold #10 styling gel to get Daniel's hair the way he would want it. Daniel could easily go through a bottle of styling gel in no time at all. Jenny and Michael agreed to go back home to get it. They knew exactly where to find it in his bathroom. In a very short time they returned.

Even now I reflect back to that afternoon as a day of such love and compassion. The afternoon viewing was full of family members who loved and cherished Daniel. We sat in the funeral parlor where Daniel's body lie and shared sweet and memorable stories about Daniel. We were even joking about Daniel's hair and how upset he must have been to see how they fixed it. All afternoon we envisioned Daniel saying, "family hurry up and get up here and do something with this hair" and how upset he must have been when he saw us pull out of the driveway at home without his Mega Hold #10 styling gel. Karl and I sat back in the room and literally watched every one of Daniel's siblings ever so lovingly give their brother their tender touches of grooming and prepping as love radiated out towards their brother. Each one had to give one final stroke or pat and give their final ok that they now approved of how he looked. At one point Joe noticed that you could tell by Daniel's pants that Daniel was not wearing a belt. When the clothes were delivered earlier no one thought of a belt because we thought the inside coverlet would come up high enough on his waist not to show his belt loops. I watched Joe take off his own belt and thread his belt in Daniel's empty belt loops. After completing the task Joe then gave a nod as to show his approval that all was well and the last physical act that he could do for his brother was completed. Karl and I sat there with this enormous amount of love for each and every one of our children including Daniel.

The evening viewing was so much more different than Karl and I had anticipated. At first we were so struck with awe by the number of people who came to see us and offer their love and condolences. There were so many people and they just kept coming. Daniel had so many of his friends come, past schoolteachers as far back as elementary school, his high school counselor, coaches, school friends from so many years past and friends from work that were three and four jobs ago. It is such a loss and a very sad loss when a child dies and a community will certainly rally around a family who has lost a child. Karl and I did very well that evening but it was only because of the spiritual experience we had that afternoon at the family viewing. We had felt so much love and compassion we wanted to pass it on. As the people filed passed us we felt their sadness and despair and we wanted them to feel what we had felt earlier but that is something that cannot be passed on. We saw that with our youngest son, Matt. We were trying so hard to do what we felt was best for Matt. We were so concerned about him and Amy and Jenny since they were in the house when Daniel was found. Karl's older brother had come from out of town and he has two sons that are one year older and one year younger than Matt. Matt had been spending lots of time with his cousins and we were thrilled for the distraction for him. Matt asked that he please be allowed to go to the beach with his cousins and not go the family viewing. Matt wanted so badly to spend all his time with the cousins. We thought this may be best and before the evening viewing we would get there early enough for me, Karl and Matt to have a private viewing for Matt. We did but it was so different than what we felt just a few short hours earlier. In hindsight we now wish we had had Matt with us in the afternoon. We wanted him to feel the comfort and peace we had felt earlier and the evening was now rushed and it did not happen for him. Knowing what I know now and knowing what our family felt in that room I would have much preferred that Matt had been with us and not gone to the beach. It was during the evening viewing that I continued to feel the people's sadness as they filed past us. I wanted them to know as I now know that life does goes on after death. Yes, Daniel's body was with us in that room but that wasn't him, that wasn't him "in that box."

The viewing was to last until 9:00 but people weren't leaving. It was 9:30 and our bishop finally asked if the immediate family could have a few minutes together before we all left to go home. We had agreed not to have an open casket at the church the next morning before the funeral service. We knew when the funeral home closed the casket that evening that they would be sealing it. Karl and I watched as grandmothers, aunts, uncles, cousins and then brothers and sisters said their final goodbyes. It was extremely difficult to watch and see so much pain and sadness in my children's faces. I knew that I wanted to be the last to see him. I brought him into the world and I wanted to be the one to send him with all my love and blessings to his next place of rest. That last act of motherhood towards Daniel would have to be the hardest thing that I have ever done in my life. To look down on this beautiful child of mine that I loved with every fiber of my being and know I would never be seeing this child again in this life was more pain than I could stand. I stood there praying for strength and hoping no one would come up and tell me it was now time to leave. The doors separating the two rooms had been closed and the hall door was closed. It was just Karl, Daniel and I in this section of the parlor. My heart could not have hurt anymore if you had pulled it out and thrown it on the floor. I could not imagine walking away from that casket and knowing I would never see him again in my lifetime. I kept asking myself how are they going to let me stay. I cannot leave him, this is my baby and I will never be able to walk away from him. His hands and body were cold but I could not stop touching him. I actually watched my tear drops fall on his fingers and hands because the grief was so unbearable in trying to deal with looking at him for the very last time. I may have been strong earlier but this was too big, far bigger and worse than I ever imagined. I did finally pull myself away and went home physically and emotionally exhausted and I had this terrible pain in my neck and right shoulder. I had been in severe pain since Sunday and I could not find any relief at all. I knew it had to be stress.

Thursday morning we woke to rain showers but Karl kept telling us it wouldn't be raining for the funeral. Family members were asking about umbrellas and raincoats and Karl kept saying you would not need them. We were enjoying his optimism because it sure was raining hard. We had planned the funeral earlier in the week with the bishop. We knew immediately whom we wanted for speakers and what music we would like to be sung. Joe had asked if he could speak. We were more than happy to have him speak at his brother's funeral. The limo showed up at the house to pick up the family members and it was not raining.

As funeral etiquette goes the family walked into the chapel last and once again the number of people who were there took me back. I could not believe how many people had stopped what they were doing in their busy lives to come to be with us. I had a close friend to tell me that seeing us walk into the chapel was the hardest part for her. Even though we are a large family it was obvious to her that someone was missing from this family. Each of the speakers did an exceptional job, but especially Joe. Karl and I were so proud of him. Joe said some wonderful and sweet things in the eulogy he gave for his younger brother.

For the first time since last Sunday we came home from the funeral to a house that was not full of people. Laurie and Missy were anxious to get back to their children who had been left with various friends since Sunday. Karl's extended family had left to go back home after the funeral. After the funeral Karl, Jenny, Amy, Matt, Joe, Michael, my mom, my brother and I went back to my house. That night after the funeral we all found ourselves in Daniel's room. The day before, Joe had bought Elton John's CD with the song Daniel. We sat and listened to that song and shared more sweet stories about Daniel. It became very obvious that there would always be songs that could easily stir emotions. It was still a sweet and very memorable evening to have the family sitting in Daniel's room sharing memories of him.

Chapter 3

The Visit

"I was feeling peace with myself"

<u>*March 25, 2003*</u>
"How long will I cry"

I walk around with this unbelievable amount of sadness and don't know what to do. I know intellectually that Daniel is dead and yet I cannot even begin to believe it. I go and sit in his room a lot. I sit in his room and cry and cry. I look at all his things and it seems so unbelievable that he isn't coming back. What am I suppose to do with all his stuff? Looking at his things is so hard for me. I keep thinking I am only 48 years old and I hope to live to be 70-80 or 90 years old. That sure is a lot of birthdays and Christmases without him. In my heart I know where he is but the pain comes from missing him so much.

Mornings are the worse. I almost hate to go to bed not because I can't go to sleep. It is because I have to wake up. Every single morning since March 2nd the very first thought that comes to my head is Daniel is dead. As soon as I open my eyes that is my first thought. It is such a horrible jolt to my body. You truly do hate to go to sleep because you know you are going to have that jolt of reality immediately when you awaken. It almost feels as if it would be easier if you just always stayed awake. If you were already awake then you never would have to go through that dramatic jolt to your system of your mind reminding you that Daniel is dead. Of course the problem is that physically this is impossible. I also have to overcome a very difficult habit. Before Daniel died I would lie in bed and listen for his little black Toyota MR2 sports car to turn the corner. I would then listen for the front door and know he was safely home. Some nights I would doze off and when I awoke in the middle of the night I would always go and check on him. I would either go to the front window to make sure his car was parked out front or sometimes I would go to his room to make sure he was sleeping in his bed. I always slept better when I knew everyone was safely home. But there are mornings now that I awake and I suddenly realize that I didn't hear Daniel's car or hear the front door during the night then the massive jolt of reality hits me. Then instantly I remember he is dead and won't be coming in the front door again. It's this morning jolt that saddens me so deeply. So I cry every morning and then manage to get out of bed.

April 10, 2003
"The first dream"

Last night I had my first dream about Daniel since he died. It was a strange sort of dream and yet I loved it because it was as if I saw him and heard his voice. It was almost as if I had a visit with him. Daniel came to me in full battle Army fatigues. He was even wearing the hard helmet. I was so happy to see him. I knew he was dead and yet we never discussed that part. I said, "Daniel, are you all right?" He was so emphatic in his answer when he answered, "yes, Mom." I questioned him again by asking, "are you sure you are all right." The second reply was "yes, Mom I am fine." I then woke myself up because I reached out and touched him. I had such happiness and joy in seeing him and knowing he was ok. At the very end of the dream I was crying tears of happiness. When I awoke I realized it was all a dream and I wasn't really with him so I cried. I turned my face down into my pillow so as not to disturb Karl who was sleeping next to me. I was so sad it was only a dream. I wanted to hurry up and go back to sleep to see if I could resume my dream where I had left it when I woke myself up. I fell back to sleep but did not dream of Daniel again. This morning I could not wait to tell Karl about my Daniel dream. I realized as I was telling him that it was such a fresh vivid picture I had had of Daniel. He spoke to me and I remembered his voice so easily. I also remembered that I had cried when I awoke in the night only because it was a dream and not the real Daniel. Now with the morning light and a clear head I want to dream about him again and again. I want to see him again so clearly and hear his voice, but now I must settle for a visit in a dream world.

April 18, 2003
"Mom, let me go"

Last night was the most emotional night I have had since Daniel died other than the horrific day of his death. Karl had business partners that were scheduled to come over in the evening at 7:00. I had had an unusually hard day and felt as though the walls were caving in on me. I prepared the downstairs for the guests and knew there was no way I could actually go in and sit amongst them and act like any kind of a decent host. I knew my best bet was to stay away. I greeted the guests and made my apologies and said that I was helping Matt with a homework assignment. An hour later at 8:00 I felt as if I was going to scream. I felt as though everything was crashing in on top of me. I tried so hard to distract myself from the noise of the guests in our family room. I was amazed that Karl was able to carry on what sounded like a fairly intelligent conversation with them. I had no idea how he was able to stay focused. There was laughter coming from the room and such meaningless trivial conversations. It was becoming more than I could stand. I wanted to know what there was to laugh about. I heard someone complain about a very simple matter that I knew was of no significance. I thought to myself you think that's a problem and you are so worried about that. You've got to be kidding. Let me tell you what a problem is. I knew I needed to get some fresh air and I decided to go for a walk. I decided I would head towards the nearby middle school and walk around the outside track. The middle school is a very short distance from our house especially if you go to the back of the school where the track is located. I had only gone a short distance from the house before I began to cry, which felt like a pressure gauge being released. I decided I would walk and cry until I couldn't cry anymore. As long as I was crying I would keep walking and only when I stopped crying would I begin my journey back home. I have heard of the "Trail of Tears" but I was on the track of tears. I was the only one out there. That was probably a good thing. I walked and cried and cried and walked circle after circle on that track. I did lots of talking with Daniel. I asked him if he knew where I was. If he even knew I was at his old middle school on the track that he had run on as a young boy. I wanted to know if he was aware that I was there that night and grieving so hard for him. I called out to him and God that I couldn't do this. I could not go on and I was sure that I was not going to make it. The pain I was feeling was too severe for any human being to bear. I was pleading and begging for God to sustain me. I had always heard that God would never give you more than you could stand and I was letting him know that this was too much. I just could not do it. The loss of one of my children was truly destroying me. I was racked with so much pain and suffering that I felt as though I had been reduced to a mere portion of what I had been before March 2nd. As I continued to walk around the track I continued with my conversation to Daniel. I was able to pour out my heart to him. I expressed how much I missed him and loved him. I also felt very compelled to tell him that I had forgiven him and I was not angry with him. I talked with him as if he was only inches away and we were literally walking the track together. I also told him that I knew he had been in so much pain that Sunday morning and I was beginning to see the cause. I told him that I knew he had gone to an emotional place he had never been before that Sunday morning and he did not know how to get back. I was very aware of the fact that if he could have just seen the aftermath from this tragic loss that he would have never gone through with it. It wasn't death he was trying to find but he was desperately trying to escape the pain. I also told him that I would never accept or fully understand why he took his own life but there were now some answers that had not been there earlier.

I was feeling peace with myself and was relieved that the heart wrenching sobs were coming to a halt. I was finally gaining composure and actually felt very good about the very one-sided conversation I had had with Daniel. It felt very therapeutic to say those thoughts out loud and get them all out in the open. It felt good and satisfying that I was offering a very honest expression of forgiveness to Daniel. I also felt the very familiar assurance that once again I was not alone and the Lord was very much aware of my pain. I saw on my watch that it was nearly 10:00. I could not believe that I had been walking around that track for nearly 2 hours. I was ready to head back home but decided to make one more circle. I was hoping that a little bit of extra time would insure that our guests had left our house. I knew I had been crying very hard for a long time and I did not want to run into them as they were leaving and I was coming in. I was sure my eyes were red and swollen. All my crying had ceased and I was actually noticing what a beautiful night it had turned out to be. The skies were clear and the stars were bright. I was surprised how lost I had become in my grieving that I had not even noticed the skies, not even once. My mind was going over all the things that I needed to do the next morning. I was thinking what I could do before I went to bed to help make tomorrow morning run a little more smoothly. Daniel was not on my mind because my mind was racing with my "to do" list. As I turned the last curve at the end of the track I heard Daniel's voice. Once again I am very startled and have no idea where it is coming from. It is definitely his voice and it is a soft and very gentle tone. I turn because I am positive that I will see him standing directly by my side. I see nothing but I heard Daniel's voice and it said, "Mom, let me go." I immediately stopped walking and say, "Oh, my God, is that really you Daniel?" I knew instantly that it was him and yet I have no physical proof that would ever support this statement. I look in the grass circle that is surrounded by the track. I see a metal form that is sitting on the grass at the edge of the track. I know it is one of those well-padded forms that football player's use when they are practicing their rushing drills. I was so glad that it was only a few steps from me. I take hold of the metal form and hold on. I feel as though my knees are about to buckle under me. I cry out loud, "Daniel don't ask me to do this. I will never be able to let you go. Please don't ask me to do something I know I cannot do." I am crying because it is such a shock to know he is right there with me on the middle school track. Daniel says again, "Mom, let me go. I come to you every time you grieve so hard and you must let me go so I can become exalted." I began to pour out my heart to God, as I have never done in my entire life. Begged doesn't sound as though it was a strong enough word but that is the only word to come to mind as to what I was doing? Begging and pleading to God. "Oh God, please help me to know and confirm to me that I am really feeling Daniel's presence and he is asking that I let him go." Immediately there was a warmth and feeling of such assurance that spread from the top of my head to the soles of my feet. I knew I had just received my answer. Daniel was asking his mother to let him go. I have had the impression on several occasions since March 2nd that Daniel is going to be sad as long as we are sad. I knew I had felt him near me on so many occasions. Now I feel as though I've been told that he comes to me when I have these heart wrenching grieving sobs. He wants so much to be a comfort to me and to give his mother love and compassion. However, I have been calling on him so much that he is being taken from his eternal journey of preparing and doing the work that he needs to be doing now. It feels as though I am holding him back from some very important work because he feels such a need to be with me. I finally said, "I can make no promises because my pain is so great right now but I would make a very sincere attempt in trying." When I returned home I was so glad to see that there were no extra cars parked out front. I came in and went straight to my bedroom. When I turned on my bathroom light I was so surprised to see my reflection in the mirror. Half way down from the top of my blue shirt to the middle I saw that my shirt was wet. I had cried so hard that my tears had soaked one half of the front of my tee shirt. So between the extra long time of walking around the track and crying I was very physically and emotionally exhausted. I said goodnight to the family and went to bed where I very quickly fell asleep.

April 25, 2003
"Good days and bad days"

It has been a few days since I last wrote. I wanted to write because there are so many thoughts and memories going through my head. I feel as though I may forget yet I feel such pain that I can't imagine how I would ever forget these feelings and yet I am afraid if I don't write them down then I may forget.

The aching in my heart is no different than it was March 2nd or the last time I wrote. It is truly a physically pain. It's not like a heart attack but I now know what it feels like to have a "broken heart." Those two little words have a new meaning to me and so does the phrase "dying of a broken heart." I have since read that when a body goes through a tragic loss that somewhere in your body you will feel a very physical pain. Your body cannot physically hold in so much pain and misery. On March 2nd my physical pain was definitely in my neck and right shoulder. I would stand under very hot showers, rub my neck with ointments for strained muscles, and I would ask people for neck rubs. I was never able to receive any relief until weeks after the funeral and it wasn't from any thing I did to relieve the pain. It was as if the pain left with no notice just as it arrived with no warnings. But this aching in my heart today is very different from that neck and shoulder pain I felt when Daniel died. I feel as if I am in a fog. I know I attended a funeral and yet this is so incomprehensible to me that I have a child who is dead. It feels like a physical weight that is sitting on my chest all the time. My heart is broken.

I remember the first day that I thought I went the entire day and didn't cry. It was April 13th. I was feeling so proud of myself not because I hadn't cried that day but perhaps I was healing. I was saying my prayers late that evening. It was a prayer of gratitude that perhaps there was a slight movement in my grieving process. I remember so well telling Heavenly Father that I wasn't sure how things worked but I needed Him to give Daniel a message. Please tell him I was ok and I was going to make it. And for some reason I started crying because I realized how desperately I wanted to talk to Daniel and see him again. I wanted to give him the message myself and tell him how much I loved him. Then I felt sad because I now realized I hadn't gone a day yet without crying. I once had someone who has experienced the same loss with her son tell me that she cried everyday for 6 months. I sure feel as though I am right on target for the same time line.

Some days are better than others in that the crying isn't one of those heart wrenching long sobbing crying spells. Yet they are the quick teary eyed crying spells where tears run down your cheeks and it last a short time. You are grateful for those short little cries because they don't draw your body to total exhaustion. But there is a definite drawback to the so-called little crying spells. They hit you with absolutely no warning. You are totally broadsided and you have no way to prepare for them. It can be the smallest thing that catches you totally unprepared. In the last few weeks it has occurred several times. I remember the first one very well. I had to go to Wal-Mart to buy the dog some food. I had a definite purpose and this was going to be a very short, well-planned trip. I entered the door at the bakery section. As I was pushing my cart I grabbed a pastry and tossed it in my basket. As it made the all too familiar sound of hitting the bottom of the shopping basket I came to a complete stop. I had grabbed a favorite food of Daniel's as I had done so many other countless times. It was such a favorite of his that I never went to Wal-Mart without buying it for him because he just enjoyed it so much. As I saw it laying in the cart my eyes began to burn and the tears welled up and came running down my cheeks. I slowly picked up the pastry and placed it back on the shelf. I realized that I would never have the joy of buying that for him again. So there I stood in the middle of a Wal-Mart store at 8:00 in the morning with warm tears soaking my face. I remember people looking at me but I couldn't stop the tears. I had certainly been broadsided by that one.

As strange as it sounds you appreciate the good days. The good days are when you start to cry but can compose yourself rather quickly and pull yourself together after a rather short cry. You learn to appreciate these types of days because first of all there aren't very many of those days and what I have now labeled as a bad day is a really bad day. It is almost as though when I first wake up I can tell what kind of day it's going to be. There doesn't seem to be any rhyme or reason for what can make an ordinary day turn into a bad day. Some days it feels as though the pain and sadness just keeps bubbling up to the surface. For some reason that I haven't quite figured out yet I can shove it back down a couple of times but then you reach the point when you know you can't shove it down anymore and the flood gates burst open. There is no way to gain control or stop it. These soul-wrenching cries last a long time and for me it has always been the Comforter who comes to my rescue and pulls me back from such utter despair. Once I am what I call "back" I am completely back and I know my eyes will be dry for a while. I just wish I knew what triggers these awful mournful cries versus the little short crying spell.

There are lots of days that I think there isn't a tear left in my body. I knew I would become dehydrated if I cried any longer and yet I can manage to cry more. I had no idea grieving was such hard work. I have read that mental health care professionals feel it takes a full 2 years before anything will seem normal. Other professionals have stated that it can easily take 7 years of hard grieving for a child. I cannot imagine feeling this way for seven long years. This is definitely the hardest thing that I have ever done in my life. People are constantly telling me that they have no idea how I do it. They can't even imagine losing a child. I usually say to myself when I hear those type of comments, you are right. It is the worse thing that can happen to you. Just imagine the very worst thing that can happen to you and it's still worse than you could ever imagine.

Last week I was very innocently looking for something in the garage. Daniel's car is still there because Daniel had been working on it even up to the night before he died. As I entered the garage from the breakfast nook I froze on the stairs. I had caught a glimpse of a small yellow piece of paper that was lying on his dashboard. I opened his car door, took out the yellow piece of paper and cried. It had nothing to do with what was on the piece of paper. In fact I don't even remember what was written on the paper. The words had no real meaning. It had nothing to do with what was written on the note. I cried because it was a note written in Daniel's very own distinct handwriting. In fact it was a very long time before I could ever get the courage to look at the suicide note he had left us. It wasn't because I feared what it would say. Karl had already told me everything the note said. I was afraid of not being able to look at his handwriting. Those tiny little letters he wrote that made his handwriting so distinctively unique. So I stood in the garage and wept as I looked at a tiny piece of paper, which had words on it but had no meaning. I keep telling myself I went to a funeral but I still cannot believe my child is dead.

<u>April 26, 2003</u>
"What if?"

On today's entry of my original journal I have two tiny pieces of splintered wood glued to the top of the page. The entry begins with: Why would I want to put little pieces of splintered wood in this journal? These little pieces of wood are what unlocked such a large piece of the puzzle of why. These are splinters that are taken from the closet door in Daniel's room. This morning I was folding clothes from a laundry basket that had been removed from Daniel's room. With the last piece of clothing being removed I noticed these two slivers of wood. I picked them up from the bottom of the basket and I knew immediately what these pieces were and where they had come from. I tossed them on my end table beside my bed and they landed on top of my journal. Tonight I decided to glue them on the top of the page.

I suppose that I need to fill in a lot of gaps before I start writing about a splintered closet door. Daniel has a friend who he has known since seventh grade. These two guys were the best of friends. They saw each other nearly everyday for years and years. If they didn't actually make a visit then they talked on the phone. This friend lives on the street next to ours. In middle school they walked to and from school together and in high school they rode together. Daniel couldn't have loved him and cared anymore about him if he had been his own brother. One day last summer these two were at the oceanfront in the town we live in. There is nothing unusual about that; they went to the beach all the time. But I have played the "what if" game with this particular beach trip a million times since Daniel's death. "What if" he hadn't gone to the beach that day and had gone the day before or the day after. "What if" he had gone to the beach a couple of hours earlier or a couple of hours later? The "what if" game is played out on this particular beach trip because Daniel met a girl that day. Their chance meeting that day is by such mere circumstance of the two of them being there at the exact same moment. The variable of them meeting could have been off by as little as minutes and if that were the case then he would have never met her.

Chapter 4

Month 3

"The Fog"

<u>May 5, 2003</u>
"Why?"

I write in this journal because of the much needed healing this journal brings me. I write because I want so much to be reading my journal at a future date and see healing and know my grief is different than it was in 2003. I write because I truly hope in twenty, thirty, or more years I can look at Daniel's suicide and have more answers or acceptance. I will hope more answers will be known but I know it's not very likely. Karl tells me that if Daniel were to stand in front of me today and tell me why I still would not understand or accept his answer. I would still be unhappy with the reason. So in years to come I hope healing comes. I want to reach a point where I have found peace. I want to no longer be plagued by the whys because I will never know the whys.

It has been a couple of days since the 2-month anniversary. I find no relief from the fog that hangs so heavily over my head. I go through these daily motions and at night I can't remember what I've done that day. I am so glad I have my planner because this is what tells me what I need to do the next day and tells me what I did that day. Trying to have any kind of decent conversation is so difficult for me. I try so hard to keep people from knowing that I am straining to pay attention. It's not because I don't like the person or not enjoying their company it's because this fog I am in keeps me from being able to focus.

Thoughts and insights do manage to emerge from the dense fog and some things make a little more sense. I believe with all my heart and soul that Daniel's choice to take his life was Daniel's choice. Of course it was a very bad choice. He was so limited in his ability to make a rational decision because of the pain he was in. It was his choice to take his life, but he is dead because of a girl. He loved that girl so much. It was his first love, first girlfriend, and first girl to ever have that much of an emotional hold on him. I can remember Valentine's Day a few short weeks before he took his life. He had never bought a girl a Valentine's present before and didn't realize he should have put in his flower order earlier than Valentine's Day afternoon and also purchased the card earlier. When he went to the Hallmark store I told him to be prepared for things to be really picked over. When he came back he told me there were no cards left that he liked so he found one with a nice picture on the front and it was blank on the inside and he would write something. As he was preparing to leave to go have dinner with her he seemed quite concerned that he didn't know what to write in her card. I looked at him and said, "Daniel, you don't want you mother writing your Valentine's Day card to your girlfriend." But he said, "Mom I need help because I don't know what to put." I looked at him, and said, "Daniel, do you love her?" He looked me in the eyes and said, "Of course I do." I then said, "Well, tell her, its Valentine's Day." I knew then he cared a great deal about this girl. Teenage boys at that age don't know how to express themselves very well and I am sure this was the case with Daniel. He adored her and it would not surprise me in the least that he was overwhelming and probably smothering the girl. She probably felt as though she had no breathing room. I can only guess that at her young age she wanted to date other boys and have more time with her girlfriends. So when she broke up with him I know he felt as though he couldn't go on and he had nothing to live for. He had told me once that he felt she was the one that he would want to marry someday. He was definitely thinking very long range with her and for this relationship to come to an abrupt end was more than he could stand. He could not imagine living if she wasn't a part of his life.

Daniel had a black Toyota 1991 MR2. He loved that car. He loved it so much that he had a picture of that car in his wallet. The last week in January 2003 the car had broken and Daniel had been working and working on that car in our garage. Karl and I were so thrilled with what he had done. He had taken the car completely apart and repaired it and was in the process of putting it back together. Daniel and his best friend had worked on the car all day and night the day before he died. He had done so much work on the car and was nearly finished. On the Saturday before he died he was beginning to put the fluids back into the car. That night Karl and I had taken an out of town business guest to dinner. When we got home at 10:30 Daniel was telling his dad about how much work he had gotten done. He was so excited that he was getting closer to driving that car again. He wanted to drive it again so badly and the finished project was in sight. Daniel was in a good mood because he was so happy with all the work he had been able to accomplish. This was definitely not the mood of a kid who wanted to kill himself. He wanted that car running and to be out driving the streets again. Karl and I went to bed around 11:00 and his best friend left to go home shortly after that. He said Daniel was fine and never said a thing about anything being wrong the entire day. We have since discovered she broke up with him and our time line makes it happen between the time we went to bed Saturday night and finding him dead in his room Sunday afternoon. Friends of Daniel have told us that they knew she was going to break up with him that weekend but Daniel didn't know.

There are few pieces of the puzzle that are missing but some things have been found that help us understand what happened that Sunday morning. On the following Monday morning after his death it was discovered that a poster on the inside of Daniel's closet door had small rips in it. Karl also discovered that there were very small drops of blood on the poster. When the poster was taken down it was discovered that the inside of his closet door had been repeatedly pounded over and over again. It had been hit so hard that the door had holes and the wood was splintered. These are the same splinters that I found in the laundry basket that I glued in my journal. This is a very solid strong wooden door that Daniel had managed to punch holes in. At the family viewing on Wednesday we all noticed that his right hand was broken. His knuckles were huge and so swollen. The funeral home had attempted to cover the scrapes and bruises on his knuckles with make-up. This also explained the tiny spots of blood on the poster. The splintered wood from the door had cut his right hand. His closet door was a huge example of Daniel going to a place he had never been before. Daniel never got angry and lost control. I have never heard him raise his voice at any person. For

Daniel to hit a wooden door so hard that he broke his hand and splintered his door makes me realize I can't even imagine the feeling of rage he must have been in. He was so devastated by the news of the relationship ending that he lost control of his emotions. This unbelievable amount of sadness that he must have been feeling took him to such a dark place that he saw no way out. He had to have felt as though he absolutely had no other options but to end his life. I know he lost all sense of rational thinking and he became obsessed with only one thing. He wanted to end the pain. He wasn't looking for a way to end his life as much as he was looking for a way to end the pain. Extremely limited tunnel vision took over and he saw only one option to end the pain.

There is no doubt in my mind that Daniel never meant to hurt us. Daniel was a sweet and loving person. At the viewing I can remember so many of his friends telling me they thought Daniel was the nicest guy and everyone loved Daniel. He never had an enemy and no one could remember Daniel saying a bad thing or ever talking about someone else. There were many who had also said that Daniel was the best friend they had ever had. Friends were extremely complimentary about Daniel and several friends said they had never heard Daniel use profanity in the entire time they knew him. I know if Daniel had been allowed to see the aftermath of what his tragic loss has caused he would have never gone through with it.

May18, 2003
"… my greatest trial has also given me my most spiritual experience …"

As I read over these past journal entries I see pages and pages of so much sadness and grief. There is still so much sadness today because I miss Daniel tremendously. But as I re-read these pages I am reminded of very choice blessings that I have received since his death. It some ways it feels as though I have had to have life's hardest trial to have life's choicest blessings and sweetest spiritual experiences. It sure is true that my greatest trial has also given me my most spiritual experience. No matter how sad I become because I miss him so much I can never deny what I have felt. I know that life goes on after we leave this earth and the love on the other side is just as strong if not stronger. I know Daniel is very much aware of my earthly existence and there is no denying that I have felt him near me. And for this I will always be eternally grateful.

June 1, 2003
"Looking for information"

There is one wish I had about writing this journal. I wish I had blocks of time where I could do nothing but write. I want hours and hours of uninterrupted time to write in this journal. Life gets in the way and I have to stop to attend to family or church responsibilities. It feels like forever when I get back to my journal. I write my thoughts down for two main reasons. As stated before it is very therapeutic for me to put these thoughts down on paper instead of having them go around and around in my head all the time. And secondly I sincerely hope that someone would be able to gain from my tragedy. I would pray that one day I could bring comfort to someone who suffers as I do today. In the distant future I could see myself allowing someone to borrow my journal to help another grieving mother. When Daniel first died I went to every bookstore and checked the Internet looking for books that would help me. I bought several hundred dollars worth of books on suicide. I read all the time and was desperate for information on what I was feeling. I found lots of books on suicide and books on grief. I still was not able to put my hands on what I was trying so hard to find. I had found several books written by different women whose husbands had killed themselves. I wanted a book from a mother's perspective. I wanted to know how a mother felt and what she experienced. There isn't enough information out there for parents of children who have killed themselves.

June 2, 2003
"Families can be together forever"

Three months today! It can't be possible that is has been only three months. Three months is a summer, three months is a season and it feels forever since all this senseless tragedy began.

The first week-end in April was general conference for our church. A very well known and loved general authority that is a member of the First Presidency gave a talk. President James E. Faust's talk made Karl and me feel as though he was speaking directly to us for our behalf. His talk came at the two month anniversary of Daniel's death. We both cried when we heard the talk even though there were hundreds and hundreds of miles between us. We still felt as though he had prepared that talk just for our ears. He spoke of children and the sealing powers that parents have with their children. He spoke of the greatness that these powers hold even after death. He explained the eternal blessings of Christ's atonement and how the blessings of the atonement carry over to the other side of the veil to our beloved children even after death. This talk gave Karl and me such comfort, hope and more confirmation that we will indeed live with Daniel again forever. Daniel is still ours and we are very much an eternal family. Several weeks ago we learned that this general authority would be visiting our area for an area conference. Our stake president was very aware of how much this talk had meant to both of us. With the help of our stake president we were able to meet with President Faust on Saturday evening. Karl and I wanted to give him our personal and very heartfelt feelings of thanks we had for him because of his talk. President Faust is a very busy man with an extremely busy schedule especially on an area conference weekend like the one he was attending. When we entered the room where President Faust was to meet us, Karl and I had never and I want to emphasize never felt such love as we did when President Faust greeted us. Karl entered the room first and as Karl extended his arm to shake his hand President Faust took him in his arms and embraced him. He kept hugging him for a long time. Then he embraced me. We all sat in a circle facing each other. President Faust began with two scriptures. The first was from the Book of Mormon, Alma 7:11-12 and Doctrine and Covenants 138:58-59. He spoke of the not knowing the whys meaning the not knowing why people take their lives. He spoke of the imbalance they have in their brain chemistry. It was at this point that the conversation turned. It became very obvious that this meeting was not going to be about Daniel but about us, the parents, the living. We had brought a picture of Daniel that we showed him because we wanted him to see our beautiful son that we had so much grief for. He cried as he looked at Daniel's picture and he expressed what a beautiful young man this was. We talked for about 15 more minutes. President Faust then asked what he could do for us. Karl asked that he give me a blessing. For over a week we knew this meeting was going to take place and we were very excited and concerned that we not waste one minute of his precious time. I had been praying that I receive any information regarding our upcoming meeting. I felt very strongly that I should ask for a prayer while we were with him. Now I am thrilled when he so willingly gave his approval and said he would love to give me a blessing and he would lay his hands on my head. This blessing was sweet and full of so much love and comfort. At the beginning he told me I had been and am a very good mother who taught her children truth and light. That one little statement was very meaningful and very insightful to me. I have prayed and prayed for months wanting to know if it is my fault that Daniel died. I had to know if I had failed Daniel in some way and if I could have done more to prevent this horrible tragedy. Only God knew what was in my heart. I had prayed so many times. I had even fasted last Sunday and again on Wednesday that I would receive an answer but no one knew of this prayer in my heart but God. So as President Faust began by telling me that I was a good mother and had taught my children truth and light I knew for sure the Lord was using President Faust as a mouthpiece to speak through him to me. I knew only the Lord knew the true desires in my heart that night. A few other key points of the blessings were that Karl and I were to keep our temple marriage and sealing strong, nurture this marriage during this difficult trial. We were told to look forward and not backwards and by looking forward the bad memories will go away and will be replaced with only good memories. He also said that all blessings I had ever received before and even including my Patriarchal Blessing were now as if they were just given to me that evening. All past blessings of my life were to be evoked and come forth now and he ended with how much the Lord loves me. As our meeting ended we all embraced again and once again I must write that I have never felt such un-conditional love as we did that night. There was so much love given to Karl and me. We were like strangers to him but we still felt so much love from him. I will spend the rest of my life and probably into eternity trying to acquire that same beautiful and amazing characteristic of unconditional love towards another human being. I never witnessed such a perfect example of Christ-like love as was displayed to Karl and myself from President Faust.

I am so grateful for this choice blessing to have been in the presence of such a spiritual giant and yet I have a twinge of sadness too. The sadness is because it took the death of my son to have had this meeting. I was sad as President Faust looked at Daniel's picture and cried. I thought Daniel you have a prophet of the Lord looking at your picture and crying because you are dead. In the back of my hand written journal is a letter from Elder M. Russell Ballard. An apostle of the Lord wrote a personal letter to me because Daniel is dead. In 1987 Elder Ballard had written this wonderful talk on suicide, "Things we know and don't know." It gives me such comfort and peace every time I read it. A month after Daniel died I wrote Elder Ballard a thank you note. I wrote the note expressing my thanks to him. I told him how thankful I was for his listening to the still small voice when he wrote that talk. I never thought or expected him to take the time to write me back. These are extremely busy men who need to be serving in so many places. And yes I am very grateful for the very special and personal reply I got from Elder Ballard. I am very grateful for these blessings that have come my way but I have to say I would without a moments hesitation give them all back if I could have Daniel living in my life again. I would give back anything that has been given to me for comfort and peace. Just please give me my Daniel.

Chapter 5

Months 4 & 5

"Coping"

June 16, 2003
"I feel the need to write"

Isn't it interesting that at three months I hit a brick wall. I have no idea why. I feel as though I am coasting along in my routines of daily life. One day I feel as though I am surviving and then the next day, "bam", I feel as though I can't function and life is so hard. I have no idea if that is normal in this journey of grief. No, I take those words back. Of course it's not normal. There is absolutely nothing normal about any of this since March 2nd. A few hours ago I was sitting in traffic at a red light. Out of nowhere comes this thought that I cannot believe I have a son who is dead and even worse is I cannot believe I have a son who killed himself. Am I still in such denial? Have I not yet fully accepted this? It feels as though there may be a piece of me that is refusing to accept it or will ever accept it. Today my heart tells me that I will never accept his death.

Karl and I have talked at great lengths that we will never get over this. We will just learn to cope with it. We will have to learn new coping skills to get through this. The three-month anniversary was extremely hard for me. I cried so hard everyday for the entire week of the anniversary death date. I tried so hard to distract myself but nothing seemed to work. I miss him so much and each day and each week I feel as though the hole in my heart is getting bigger and bigger.

I am going to try to be more diligent in my journal writing. I certainly have lots of emotions and feelings right now in regards to how much I am missing Daniel. I feel the need to write so I can put these feelings on paper but it is hard to find the energy. I am trying to distract myself constantly with busy work and writing in my journal puts me center stage right in the middle of my sadness and pain.

June 21, 2003
"Can I help others?"

I go to therapy twice a month and I am not sure if I am getting out of these sessions what I need to be getting. I do like that it is a place where I can talk about Daniel as much as I want. There seems to be so many people that make me feel as though I am walking on eggshells when I am around them. I can come in their presence and I feel immediately that they have fear but of what I am not completely sure. I think they are afraid that I might cry in their presence. Afraid that I might bring the subject of Daniel up and then they won't know what to say. I even get the feelings that they are so afraid that they may accidentally say something to make me start thinking about Daniel or say something that will make me cry. Don't they know I think about Daniel 24/7? He never leaves my mind. It's not like they could ever say anything that would trigger me into thinking about Daniel. I am already sad and there is no way that anyone would ever be able to say something that would make me sad. I love it so much when people bring the subject of Daniel up themselves. For me that means they haven't forgotten about him. I love it when people ask how I am doing and truly mean it. I like it when people let me talk about Daniel and seem to have a favorable interest. I could talk about Daniel non-stop if I just had an audience. There are times when I have to be so aware of what's going on around me. Daniel is always on my mind and it feels as though the thought I am having of Daniel is right on the tip of my tongue. It would be so easy to just start blurting out some thought that I am currently having of Daniel. If I am involved in a conversation and it doesn't matter if it is one person or a room full of several people I must be very attentive. I fear that I will just start talking about Daniel even though no one else has even mentioned him. The thoughts of him are always in the forefront of my mind so it would be so easy to start talking about him.

So, going to counseling is good because it is a place where I can do lots of talking about Daniel. Today I was telling my therapist about this dream that I have had several times. It is a very real and very detailed dream. It is about Daniel yet he isn't actually in the dream. I am standing on what appears to be a high school auditorium stage. The auditorium is full of teenagers. I am not standing behind a podium but I am walking from side to side on the stage. Behind me is a huge drop down screen. On the screen is the PowerPoint presentation of Daniel's pictures that Karl made for Daniel's viewing. I am on this stage in a very nice royal blue suit telling the audience, "Don't do it! Don't ever do this to your parents. Killing yourself is never the answer and it can never be an option. You think it won't matter but the aftermath of what you will leave for your parents to deal with will be so horrible for them. You can never imagine the sadness, grief and pain this causes the survivors of suicide." In this dream as I am walking back and forth across the stage I see that I have this audience in the palm of my hands. I have a very captivated audience and all I can think of is that I have to get through to them. Even if I save one it will be worth it. I always enjoy dreaming this dream because I feel so much purpose and service out of something that was so terrible and tragic in my life.

July 10, 2003
"We all grieve differently"

There seems to be so much that is going on around me physically and mentally. There have been so many emotions in the last couple of weeks. It almost seems that there is so much that I won't be able to put it all on paper. I'll start with what has been the biggest issue. It has been consuming all my thoughts and feelings but I was not able to write about it. There was a rift that was pulling Karl and me apart. We were both very much aware of it and almost didn't care either. We were so consumed with our own personal grief and emotions that we wouldn't take the time to see if we were meeting each other's needs.

By some very unusual circumstances Karl became owner of a sailing school and sailboat chartering service in this very large area we live in. Now this process all began on the 18th of February. It was all in the early preliminary stages at the time of Daniel's death. Of course everything stopped for about 4 or 5 weeks after Daniel's death. It was mid-April that he began to take an active part in putting this new adventure all together. I was happy for him. I was especially happy for him that he had a distraction. Sailing is Karl's passion and has been ever since he was a young boy. He loves sailing so much and I truly was happy for him that he had something to take his mind off of the pain we were feeling. I began to notice something was happening. Karl was spending an enormous amount time with the sailing school and loved it! Now the reasons of resentment begin to build in me and the resentment begins to turn into anger. I can't stand how I am feeling. Am I being this very self-centered wife who resents her husband for having something that can distract him and I don't have anything. My feelings being right or wrong aren't the issue for me. My issue is that I am even having these feelings of anger and resentment. I am having these feelings that I don't like and I don't know what to do about it. As I sit here now and write I can see both sides from a totally different point of view and also from a rational point. But a few short weeks ago I had not reached this point in my thinking. What mattered then was that I felt hurt and rejected.

I still want to talk about Daniel all the time. I feel like my friends and family are tired of my "Daniel" stories. I feel like no one wants to hear "one more Daniel story." What is worst is that I now feel as though the worst has happened. I feel as though Karl doesn't want to talk or hear about Daniel either. I am crushed and totally at a loss. I have always had Karl to talk to about Daniel anytime day or night. I sense that he feels annoyed or irritated that I am bringing him up again. On more than one occasion I have noticed that he quickly changes the conversation or he shuts down and won't talk at all. I now find myself hating the sailing school and I do mean hating it. I hate that his cell phone rings non-stop. He is either physically at the marina or he is on the phone all the time with someone who wants information about the school. Perhaps at an earlier time Karl may have felt torn between the sailing school and me but now I know that I have lost. The sad part is I lost before I even knew I was competing. Karl and I have always had a great marriage. It has always been a marriage full of love and lots of devotion and attention given to each other. We met and fell in love the summer Karl graduated from high school. So it has been 29 wonderful years of a love that has grown and matured over the years.

The first week of June I realized that I was a very unhappy woman with my relationship towards Karl. I try to think rational but at this point it does not matter to me if my feelings are right or wrong, logical or illogical. The problem is that the feelings were there and I had no idea what to do. In my 29 years of marriage I have never dealt with negative emotions pertaining to my marriage. Not only were these feelings new but they were very scary feelings because they were very unfamiliar feelings towards Karl.

I knew that Matt was leaving for scout camp on June 22nd. I decided to take advantage of this opportunity and go to my mother's while he is at camp. No one knows the real reason I am leaving to go to my mom's which is I am actually running from my marriage. I have not seen my mother since she was here for Daniel's funeral. The week I was there was a good week and a not so good week.

I loved having the one on one time with my mother. I enjoyed that part so much but I was having a difficult time there. At first I thought it was Daniel. Here I was at my mother's and this is a place where Daniel had visited numerous times. It was once again a painful reminder of yet another place that Daniel would never visit again. My mother has pictures of the grandchildren all over her house and has had these pictures for years. As I was going through out her house I am constantly bumping into these pictures. Daniel's face always seemed to be jumping out towards me. But there was something else that was happening. I was now allowed to become very still and quiet during many parts of the day. I was no longer running the roads taking the children to countless places through out the week. I was still and that made me think.

The second night I was there I sat in my mother's living room till 2:30 in the morning talking to my mom. We talked extensively about Daniel and I cried and cried! At one point I was crying so hard that she cradled me in her arms as if I was a small child and she let me weep on her shoulder. It had been a while since I had wept that hard and long. It made me realize I still have so much pain and sadness inside of me. Those feelings are still just as raw and painful as they were four months ago when all this sadness began. Since I had the time to be still and quiet I now had the opportunity to reflect and think a lot about Karl and me.

I was talking to him on a daily basis but it was nothing more than a superficial conversation of me checking in to see how he and the children were doing. While I am doing all this reflective thinking I now know I have lots of resentment and anger towards him and the sailing school. It was mid-week that I emailed him and told him I really wanted to talk to him when I got back and he got back from San Diego. I flew to my mother's on June 23rd, which was on Monday, and I got back home the next Monday night, the 30th. Karl left for a business trip to San Diego on Monday morning the 30th. I had also planned my trip around his trip. I made sure I got back home after he had left for San Diego. I figured more days apart would be all the better. Karl would be home Thursday morning of the week I got back. In my email I asked that we please talk when he got home. I wanted to do it in person and not over the phone or the Internet. When I picked him up at the airport we didn't go home at first. We went to have lunch and to talk. We spent hours talking and it was wonderful. All my horrible misconceptions of what I thought were going on were all wrong and his misconceptions about me were all wrong.

I could now see how people could so easily have serious marriage problems when there is a death of a child. Even though we were a couple we were grieving separately and differently. Once again this is a classic example of two people who do not grieve the same way even though we were grieving over the same child, our child. There was no communication going on between us. It was such an eye opening experience for both of us. We had never had problems of communicating with each other. When we weren't talking there were walls being built between us? If there is no communication then there will definitely be resentment and anger between us. It has to be all brought out and discussed or else all the emotional thoughts we are harboring inside will only fester into something bigger. We are both extremely emotional and our emotions are raw and our emotions are being worn on our sleeves right now. We decided to do lots more nurturing towards each other and be there more for each other. It felt so good to finally talk and to know he wasn't feeling the way that I was so sure he was feeling. I have learned a very valuable lesson to never assume how someone else is feeling unless you ask him or her yourself. It feels so beautiful to have the peace and love back into this very special marriage. I love him with all my heart and can never imagine going through the loss of Daniel without him.

July 21, 2003
"A strange new feeling"

A strange and new feeling is going on now. Just when you think you have gone through all the feelings and emotions that could possibly go along with grief a new one suddenly appears. I don't like this one. I am very scared of this one because it is a massive amount of fear that has taken over my once somewhat rational mind. This fear is gripping and paralyzing and I find my ability to go through a typical day is very impaired and disturbing. It sounds silly to say that on top of all this I also have lots of frustration of not being in control. I have always been able to have control of my emotions and feelings. Sure I've been sad before but I knew it was temporary and had ways and means to pull myself out of it. This is so different and it feels as though there is no end in sight. So now what do I do? I keep trying and trying but the tears still come everyday. Then I say to myself, "just what is it that you are expecting? You have a son that has killed himself and do you think you should already be over this." When I think those rational thoughts I realize and understand why I am still crying everyday! This still does not take away from this very paralyzing fear that I am harboring lately. My fear is that this really won't ever end. I am sentenced to a life of grief and sadness because I know I will always miss him and since this feeling will never go away then I will be sad. Mothers have lost their children since the beginning of time including Eve herself. I know I am no different than all the other mothers of the world who have lost children. They have all loved their children as I love my Daniel. So I want to know are there mothers all over the world crying in their private places and yet they go on living lives that look "normal" to the rest of the world. Is there some type of secret and very private thing that all mothers experience on a daily basis and yet no one talks about it? I can't even imagine a life that is racked with so much pain that I will continue to cry everyday until my sojourn here on earth is over. Yet I know I will never stop missing him and I know I will never get over this. So the next logical thought would be that as long as I have such pain in my heart and miss him tremendously I will cry everyday. How can I be a mother to the rest of my children and a wife to Karl if my life has been taken over with grief and sadness? I have a long time to live in this world and still cry everyday. Fear, that's what I have, fear of what the future may bring. AND the little voice goes off in my head, "Why are you worrying about the future and something that you have no control over? Deal with today because you have no clue what the future has in store for you." Yea, I know easier said (thought) than done.

I think my fear is so bad today because of what I did last night. I wasn't going to include this in my journal for another type of fear. I fear what people will think and especially my family but I decided on March 9th when I wrote the first entry that I was going to write in order to help me with some much needed healing. This journal is written with brutal honesty and no glossing over. I keep telling myself in years to come when I read this journal I want to see healing in this thing called grief. So I become brave and write.

Last night I could not go to sleep. I read and watched TV and nothing was helping. The rest of the family had gone to bed early for a summertime evening. I left everyone sleeping and went for a drive around 11:30 PM. It's nearly midnight so where do I go that's open. I know Wal-Mart is open 24 hours so I go there. I walk around and find zero satisfaction in being there. I decided just to drive around for a little while longer before I headed back home. Before I realized it I was heading towards to the cemetery. There are no gates with closed entrances so I realized I could drive right in and go towards the back where Daniel's plot is located. I was hesitant at first not from fear of being in a cemetery after midnight but for personal reasons. I begin to think, what am I doing? What are you thinking? What on earth is causing you to go to the cemetery at such an unbelievable hour of the night? Why would you even go there if you know he isn't really there? Will this be the beginning of more trips to the cemetery and even trips after dark? I was crying so hard even as I was driving because I am scared. I am scared that I am losing my mind. Who else but a crazy person goes to a cemetery at 2:00 in the morning but I didn't care. I was also having another type of fear. I wasn't sure where Daniel was anymore. I began to doubt every feeling I had in the past of feeling assured in knowing where he was. All I knew for sure was the cemetery was the last place that my son's body was laid. This

I did know for sure and I had no other rational thought at the time. I wanted to go where I knew he had been last.

When I got out of my car it seemed very dark but my eyes adjusted quickly. There was actually a fair amount of light that came from a brilliant clear night. A dog started to bark very loudly. I became afraid not of the dog but that the dog's barking would wake people up in this very quiet area. There is a neighborhood that sits directly next to the cemetery on the side where Daniel is buried. I was very relieved when the dog stopped barking. I found my way to Daniel's gravesite very easily. I am not sure now if there was a moon out or not but I could read his marker very well. For a while I stood there crying so hard that I actually saw tears fall from my cheeks and hit the top of his marker. I was overcome with so much sadness. I wanted nothing more at that moment than to see, hear and touch him one more time. But in my heart I knew one more time wouldn't be enough, but oh what I would give to touch him, feel his arms around me when he gave me a hug. I wanted to hear his voice, and see that adorable little grin. I have no idea where it came from or even why I did it but I suddenly found myself lying on top of the grass that had now grown over where Daniel was buried. I lay there on my stomach with my arms out-stretched as if I were trying to hug him in the only way I knew how that night. I lay there for a few minutes and realized I would never hug him again in this life. That was a horrible dose of reality for me. What I wanted the most at that moment was not to be in this lifetime. I made myself get up and go home with the harsh reality that Daniel was indeed dead.

Chapter 6

Month 6

"Trying to regain normal"

July 27, 2003
"Finding treasures"

Twenty-one weeks ago today I lost my Daniel. I live for the day that I don't dwell on the day and can no longer remember exactly how many weeks it has been. No one in my family is aware of how painful Sundays are for me. I want to love Sundays again! I want to enjoy Sundays for being the Sabbath and not dreading Sunday as I do now every week because it's the day of the week that Daniel died. No one knows how I dread coming home from church at noon because every Sunday I begin the mental clock of reliving the Sunday afternoon that Daniel died. I try so hard to focus and become distracted with anything. I crave anything that I think might distract me. It is almost as if I have a very accurate biological clock ticking away in my head. I can be so consumed and distracted and I'll look at the clock and it's always between 2:20 and 2:30 pm. I then realize it's only a few minutes until 2:30 when it all began with the discovery of Daniel in his room.

This Sunday afternoon had an additional amount of pain for Karl and me. This afternoon we were planning to go over to Laurie's house for little Emma's two-year-old birthday party. Laurie's video camera is broken and she asked that we please bring ours. Karl got the camera out to charge the battery. He began to go through the tapes that were in the camera bag to find an empty tape so he could tape Emma's party. He accidentally found a tape of Daniel that Amy had recorded from her upstairs window. Daniel had no idea that Amy was filming him. Daniel is on the driveway putting the finishing touches on his car that he has just washed and waxed. He was also filmed taking the t-tops off and then pulling out of the driveway and driving away. Amy filmed all this and he never knew that he was being filmed. Amy was filming her room to show off her "master piece" because she had just finished painting her room. As she is filming she notices Daniel out her front windows and she began to film her brother.

Karl brings me the camera to let me see what he has discovered. I immediately notice that he has been crying. We have lots of framed pictures of Daniel in nearly every room of the house including all of the bedrooms. The siblings that still live at home wanted a picture of themselves with Daniel in their bedrooms. You become accustomed to those still pictures as best as you can. It still pains my heart greatly to look at his pictures and look at those precious eyes. It was just yesterday I was dusting Matt's bedroom dresser and cried as I moved the pictures of Daniel and Matt out of the way so I could dust. It just hurts so much to see him in a picture and know he is gone. Well, today was more pain than I imagined. This is Daniel moving, and walking. Daniel is living. It really felt like a knife stabbing in my heart. There it is again the real physical pain of a hurting heart from grief. So Karl and I both sat there and cried. We both expressed how much we would give to see him drive off in his car again. We would give anything that is humanly and earthly possible to have Daniel outside on our driveway again.

Karl and I went to our precious little granddaughter's birthday party because that's what we needed to be doing. No one there knew we had experienced such a painful and heart wrenching experience just a few short hours ago. Karl and I now know what priceless treasures these tapes have become to us. When we came home from the party Karl decided to go through the entire collection of home videos. He found several more and we realized we were craving to hear his voice. Why did he always have to clam up and become so shy? We have few videos that have his voice and those that do are only brief sentences. You can never have enough pictures and now I know it is also videos with their voices. It makes me want to make a conscious effort that the next time we are filming we are also having the people talk. People are very conscious of being put in front of a camera and they are usually embarrassed to talk. After seeing what we now don't have or will ever have; it makes me want to get lots of tape of our family's voices. We have pictures but I miss the sound of his voice so much.

August 4, 2003
"Grief vs. depression"

Last Monday I had an appointment with my therapist and today Karl met with his therapist. We each went with the intent of finding the answer to a question we both have.

We want to know how you can tell the difference between grief and depression. Two different professionals gave us both the same answer. There is a fine line that becomes very hard to tell if one has crossed over from grief into depression. It seems the body is an amazing and wonderful thing. The body will never give you more than you can stand. The loss of a child could never be given to you all at once. It's only been 22 weeks since Daniel died and that is not very long at all! Denial, shock, disbelief and numbness may be peeling away and reality is now approaching. Once again I have no way of knowing what is normal. We were both told that neither of us should expect to feel what the world calls normal feelings for at least two years in the event that you have lost a child. Also not to judge how things feel for one year or make decisions based on what we are presently feeling for one or two years. I hate it! I hate all of this! I am such an impatient person. I want this all to be over. I want to feel good again. I want to say I feel fine when people ask and I mean it because now I'm lying every time. I hate the feelings that I am feeling today. I hate myself for not being able to stop Daniel from killing himself. Today I have these flashes of anger towards Daniel but it is so short lived and very fleeting. I get angry with him for all the pain he is causing us. All this horrible, horrible pain and yet I know he too had pain. He had problems and he solved it the only way he knew how. So I don't stay mad at him very long because I know he was so sad. I do know in my heart he would have never hurt us this badly if he had known what this was going to do to his family. I know his pain is gone now. It is my hope and prayer that he is in a better place. I want his place to be a place that has the eternal perspective so he can see far enough in the future that he knows his family will be healed one day. I know Daniel will be sad as long as we are sad and I want him to be able to see far enough in the distance to see our healing process.

I go through the steps of what used to be a normal day in hopes of trying to be normal again. How abnormal is that? I am trying to act normal in a world that is now so far from being normal that it is no longer recognizable. You never want to actually wish your life away but I do wish I could fast forward my life to maybe five or ten years from now. But perhaps if I were really given that chance I would be too afraid to jump into the time traveler. How would I feel if nothing has changed and I am still just as sad? At least it does look rosier from where I am today because I have hope, lots and lots of hope. I hope that everyday gets better even if it is an ever so slight movement in feeling better.

September 4, 2003
"Going to paradise"

I would suppose in the last couple of days the best words to use that would describe my feelings would be gloomy and very melancholy. I feel as though I am on an emotional roller coaster. I am so sure of one decision and it almost feels as though only five minutes have passed and I am feeling something totally different. We got back from the big family vacation to Hawaii on Monday night. We were gone for ten days. This trip had been planned so long ago that we had even bought Daniel's ticket. This was to be the big family vacation before Daniel left to go on his two-year mission for the church. We decided to go ahead and go and we were in hopes that the excitement of the children would become a major distraction for Karl and me. Amy and Matt had never been on a plane so this would be a truly special event in their lives. I went to Paradise and yet I still cried because I miss that kid so much! This was our family vacation and I wanted so much for Daniel to be with us as a family. Our hotel room had a beautiful view of the ocean. I would find time to sit on our balcony every day so I could soak up every moment of this breath taking view. Everyday we would discover a new beach that would offer a new place to snorkel and swim. Our nights were filled with good restaurants and of course shopping with the teenage girls.

Late Sunday afternoon we were getting ready to checkout of the hotel and go to the airport for our flight back home. I decided to go out on the balcony one more time. I actually found myself out there by myself which was unusual because we all loved sitting on our balcony. As I stood there next to the railing taking in this gorgeous view I was flooded with thoughts of going home and returning back to the life we had now made for ourselves which meant a life without Daniel. I dreaded going home so much! I had no desire to leave that hotel. I knew why. Home meant pain and there is no way to escape it. I have so many painful memories at home. Yes, I still had pain and sorrow in Hawaii but everything was so different in Hawaii. Fun things to do everyday and new things to look at that had not been previously done with Daniel. I wasn't constantly saying I remember being here with Daniel or remembering something that was last done with Daniel because Daniel had never been to Hawaii. I loved the distractions.

Even the very surroundings were distractions. It was all so beautiful to look at and Daniel had never been to Hawaii. But I also knew this wasn't real and this certainly couldn't last forever. I knew if I stayed long enough it would all eventually catch up with me. I would feel just as sad and full of despair in Hawaii as I did at home.

As I stood on the balcony I realized that I had not felt Daniel's spirit one time since we were there. I had thoughts of Daniel every day we were there and I cried for Daniel everyday we were there but I never felt him to be with me. In my heart I know he is a busy boy and when I think about him in terms of what he may actually be doing there is this feeling of fear that comes over me. I stood on the balcony and said a prayer that I just needed reassurance that Daniel was ok. I get really scared sometimes and it is all based on fear. Fear takes over and I become so distressed with worry and wanting so desperately to know if Daniel is ok. I stood there and prayed oh God please remove all this fear and re-assure me that my Daniel is ok. In only a matter of seconds this beautiful white dove (not a seagull but a dove) flew directly in front of me. I quickly responded oh God please don't let me make something out of this that isn't because I certainly don't want to ever be one who appears to be seeking for a sign as my answer. I had an over whelming feeling come over me. The sweet, sweet spirit whispered to me I send you this dove to bring you peace. Your Daniel is fine. The confirmation that I felt was so strong and feelings of warmth began to go over my entire body. Such a joy of gratitude filled me and once again the Comforter had made known its presence to me.

It had only been a few days ago that Karl and I had sat together on the balcony talking about Daniel. I told Karl I truly believe in every tragedy there comes a gift and we had to look for it. I truly believe there is a gift for me. I look for it because I know it is there for me to find. I will need to search for it with eyes open because it isn't going to land in my lap. I asked Karl what he felt he had gained thus far in the last six months. He wasn't real sure but he did agree with me that the most spiritual gift we have received is the Comforter. The Comforter has come on numerous occasions to a very distraught daughter of God and has brought me comfort. I wish I were more eloquent in my ability to write. I would love to write in words what the Comforter means to me and how I feel. I have felt the spirit numerous times in my life and have recognized it for being the spirit but this is so different. I would never wish this horrible tragedy on anyone because I would never wish another human soul to experience this much pain with the death of a child. So I can only give you my heartfelt testimony that the Comforter lives and is very real. It is an incredible amount of love and peace that is conveyed through the Comforter that the Savior and Heavenly Father love me very much and are so aware of all my grief and pain. I am not alone that is for sure.

September 7, 2003
"Little secret angels"

It is another Sunday and another first Sunday of the month. Oh, when will it get any easier? When will it be Sunday as the Sabbath and not the typical response of this is Sunday the day of the week that Daniel killed himself? It being the first Sunday of the month we had all the children over for dinner. Tuesday will be Daniel's birthday. The family wanted to do something for his birthday but no one knew what to do. The older children had not been to the cemetery to see his new marker. We decided after we ate we would go to the cemetery and I would bring roses. Yesterday I bought a dozen red roses. We all went after dinner. The fifteen members of the immediate family, which included the children, their spouses and grandchildren, went to the cemetery in four cars. It felt more like a field trip than anything else. The purpose was to put flowers in the marker's vase and let those see the marker that hadn't seen it. It wasn't a time for reflection. I did notice that everyone had the same reaction that Karl and I had. You look at the marker and it is so painful to see his full name, Daniel Ryan Williams, on something as permanent as a grave marker. It is so final and unbelievably hard to look at.

There was a little black Matchbox MR2 car sitting on the marker and a small teddy bear holding a heart. It has been a few weeks since I was there but I am always amazed because there is something new and different on the marker whenever I go there. It is always a mystery because I never know who left the token gift this time. But I am so happy to know that somewhere out there in this world is someone who also misses Daniel and is thinking about him. I know it won't last much longer so I treasure the gifts that are left now. I thank my little secret angels that have not forgotten Daniel. As a mother that's my greatest fear that once Karl and I are gone who will be left to keep Daniel's memory alive and flowers on his grave. I know his siblings love him dearly but their lives are so busy and there is not the time or the feeling of need to go to the cemetery. I want it to be that way. Daniel sure isn't there. I myself don't spend time thinking about my dad's burial spot but when I go home I do think about the need to go by and leave fresh flowers. It's out of respect for the dead and not me feeling closer to my dad when I go there.

Chapter 7

Month 7

"The first birthday, anticipation is worse than the event."

September 9, 2003
"Go home; he is not here"

Today is Daniel's birthday. Daniel would have been twenty years old today. It seems funny to write, "would have been." He isn't really twenty. I know that he is frozen in my life as a nineteen year old. No matter how many years go by and how many more birthdays I spend without him he will always be the nineteen-year-old son that I lost. I must be honest and tell whoever reads this journal that spending his first birthday without him was not as hard as I had imagined. I realized that the dreading is or was worse than the actual day. I did ok and was able to reflect on some very sweet memories of Daniel and his past birthdays.

This morning after Amy and Matt went to school Jenny and I went to the florist and bought white roses. I also bought two very small balloons that are used in flower arrangements. One said, "Happy Birthday" and the other balloon said, "I love you today, tomorrow and always." While we were in Hawaii we went to the International Market and I bought a small model car that was a black MR2. It was a little larger than the Matchbox size. This model had a miniature surfboard glued on top. Today I took that to the cemetery with the white roses. This morning Jenny on her way home from her morning class had stopped and bought a birthday card. It was a really sweet card that was for a brother. I got a little teary eyed when I read the card because it made me sad that Jenny had obviously spent time picking out the right card for a brother she couldn't actually wish a happy birthday to. Jenny and I didn't stay very long and were glad to see that the red roses were holding up so well. The white roses mixed with the red roses looked lovely. I spent the rest of the morning with Jenny. Karl is in San Jose, CA this week for business.

I had a picture of Daniel that was given to me this past Sunday. It is a really good picture of Daniel. In this particular picture he has that precious, silly and cute little grin that I love so much. The picture is with a friend and the picture is good of both of them but I especially like the expression on Daniel's face. I went to a photo store to get copies made and Jenny went with me to help me crop it and enlarge it. I wanted an extra copy to send in grandmama's birthday card. I also bought a frame and put one more picture of Daniel in the house. I've lost count as to how many pictures there are now of Daniel. His pictures are found in nearly all the rooms of the house. I love to be surrounded by his pictures. I feel a closeness to him when I can see his face in so many places. I tried to fill my time on Daniel's birthday with loving memories and positive things that pertained to Daniel.

I did find myself late in the afternoon thinking about him a lot. The friend who was in the picture that I had made copies of today called me late in the afternoon. She is a freshman at Brigham Young University and is a dear friend of Daniel that cared for him greatly. She called to see how I was doing. She had been thinking about me all day. It meant so much for me to get a chance to talk to her on Daniel's birthday. I also had others to call and someone brought me a sweet and moving card and magnet for the refrigerator that talks of a mother's love. It was all special and so touching to have people care so much about me today. Everyone who called had said that they had been thinking about me since this morning. My callers felt this first birthday would be hard.

I went back out to the cemetery about 6:30 pm. I wanted to go by myself. When I got there the birthday balloon was gone. It was an extremely windy day and I know the little balloon became air borne and flew away. I was glad the balloon that expressed my love for him was still there. I felt ok being there and I felt very peaceful. I'm not sure why I went back. At first I thought I wanted to drive back to see if anyone had taken the time and took something to put on the marker. I knew lots of little treasures had been left in the past. The marker has his birthday on it so I knew there were people who knew what day it was today. I was curious to know if anyone had been there since Jenny and I had been there this morning. Ok, let's be honest here–I've promised myself complete honesty in writing this journal and that's what has to be done. I wanted to know if there would be anything left by "her." A part of me wanted to find something there because I wanted her to still care–even a little. My son loved her so much or so he thought. They weren't even together long enough to share his birthday. I am sure she knew it was his birthday. If she had gone to the cemetery then maybe she cared even a little. I hate that in my mind I've got these thoughts that Daniel is dead because of a girl who no longer cares about him and yet how absolutely stupid that sounds. Of course Daniel is dead because she no longer cared about him, that's why he couldn't imagine life without her so he ended his. I got there and found nothing new, it was the same things that were left by Jenny and me this morning.

I felt good about today and as I sat there on a nearby bench I felt good about how the day had gone. I had so dreaded this day and was very concerned because Karl would be out of town. As I sat on the bench I thought it would be nice to feel Daniel's spirit. I'm trying to rationalize these feelings by convincing myself that it is his birthday and I'm the mom. I have always been with him on his birthday for the last nineteen years. Surely I can feel his spirit on his birthday one more time. As I sat there a few more minutes I got a really big grin on my face. It felt as though I may laugh out loud. I thought Heavenly Father you certainly do have a sense of humor. I had just received this strong impression to get up and go home. Go home now! The feeling I got was, "Do you think for one minute that I am going to allow Daniel to visit you here in the cemetery? You already know he is not here. This was a place that you had to put his body and you know where Daniel is and it's not here. If you felt Daniel's spirit here you would come here all the time, looking and hoping that he would make another visit. You would be at this cemetery everyday." I thought that's exactly what I would do. I would try desperately to feel his spirit and find peace in trying to be closer to him. So I said out loud "you are right" and I got up and drove home.

As I was driving home I tried calling Karl on his cell phone and was disappointed that I had only gotten his voice mail. I wanted to see how his day had gone and was hoping it had gone as well as mine had gone today. A couple of hours later he called. It was nice to compare feelings and thoughts and to see that we had felt the same way on Daniel's birthday. We both agreed that the anticipation of the day had been far worse than the actual day. We both felt that making it though this day was a big milestone because we had dreaded it so much and were relieved it had gone well. We could now say we had lived our first "Daniel's Birthday" without Daniel. Then a couple of hours later I was watching something on TV before I went to bed. I wasn't sure what I was watching but a certain scene got my full attention. A father's daughter had died by what means I do not know. He had gone into her bedroom and started smelling her clothes in her closet. He falls apart and was crying so hard as he held her clothes to his face that he fell to the floor of her closet. I definitely got a wake up call as I viewed this TV show. Just hours ago I was thinking how well I am doing and for the first time feeling that I am actually ready to move forward. I felt as though I was making a huge step forward and perhaps I just needed to get through his birthday before I made such a big step forward. Boy, oh boy that small part of some show that I didn't even know the name of has now become a real dose of reality for me. The reason being I immediately remembered Daniel's black jacket and there was no way that I could ever go and smell that jacket now. I may have thought that I have come a long way but I still have a very long way to go. Watching those few minutes on TV made the tears flow so easily and effortlessly. The ole familiar aching in my heart was there as strong as ever and it felt as though it had never left since March 2.

September 17, 2003
"I hope dogs go to heaven"

Today I was in the mall and went by the pet store. Tomorrow is our golden retriever, Penny's birthday. Even our dog of eight years grieves for Daniel. I have felt so badly for her because I don't know if she understands that Daniel isn't coming back. Daniel loved that dog so much and spent a great deal of time with her. This dog has a weight problem because of Daniel. If Daniel had a sandwich then Penny had nearly half. Pizza and any other table food would be the same way. Daniel had no problem sharing whatever he was eating with Penny and Penny knew it. There was a very genuine love between the two of them. Penny is an incredibly loyal family member. I don't know how but for years now she will wait for everyone to come home before she goes into her bed. She lies by the front door until everyone is present and counted for. It amazes me that she always gets it right as far as her knowing who is still not at home. After the second night you can tell her that a family member is on a trip or spending the night away again and she will eventually go get in her bed. There have been several nights that the children have been at camp or left to go to college and those first couple of nights she never leaves her post by the front door. Lately there have been many nights that I go to turn off all the downstairs lights and there is Daniel's ever faithful, Penny, waiting for him. I try to tell her that I am so sorry he is gone and won't be coming back. Even though it has been six months since Daniel died she won't stay away from the front door more than a night or two before she is back at her post. A few weeks ago Daniel's best friend was here and was in the garage talking to the children. I noticed Penny getting so excited and waving her tail vigorously. She wanted in that garage immediately. I opened the door for her and she took off as quickly as she could down the steps into the garage. I noticed after a very brief amount of time she hung her head down and seemed very sad to be turning around and coming back up the steps to come inside the house again. I knew what had happened. Whenever in the past she had heard Daniel's best friend's voice it was because the friend was with Daniel. She heard his voice and knew that meant Daniel was in the garage with him. My heart broke for her and I thought, "you poor thing, you miss him just like we all do and there is no way to bring him back to us." Matt has never known a life without Penny since we got her when Matt was so young. I use to really dread the day when we no longer have Penny because these children are so attached to this dog, especially Matt. Now I'm thinking I really do hope "all dogs go to heaven" because everyone will feel better when it's time for Penny to go be with Daniel. Now that will be a happy reunion.

I went into the pet store to find a couple of Penny's favorite treats. I would love to see her happy again and maybe a favorite treat will do it. She is losing weight, which is not a particularly bad thing. I just hate she is losing it this hard way. She still has a good appetite and eats her regular dog food well. It's all of Daniel's extra goodies that she isn't eating anymore that were a lot of extra calories. As I stroll next to the pet cages I notice the most adorable beagle puppy. He is such a baby. My heart melts when our eyes make contact with each other. I ask if I can hold him. Of course they are more than willing to oblige my request. A sure sale in a pet store is a puppy in the arms of a customer. I love that this precious puppy is licking and nuzzling my neck. I'm thinking this is exactly what I need. I need something that is totally dependent upon me and I need something that I can cuddle and love on whenever I am so sad.

Now anyone who knows me will have a hard time visualizing this scene. I have never been cruel to animals. I am always the one who buys the pet food. I make the appointments and take our pets for their vet checks. I speak to Penny often and care about her well being but I have never been a hard core dog or cat lover. I have told people in the past that I do not do pets very well. I certainly do children much better. Thank goodness as I stand there I come to my senses. I realize this precious little puppy should never be tasked with making me happy again or try-ing to fill a hole in my heart that may never be filled. I am glad to be walking out of there with just doggie treats and not a puppy because there for a minute it could have gone either way.

I enter the card store on my way out of the mall to buy Karl's birthday card. On the counter I see the most adorable little stuffed lamb that is so soft. I can't believe how soft and cuddly this little stuffed animal feels. I buy it! It is a reminder for me to never forget how close I came to buying a living animal. If I need to cuddle and love on something it has to be the little lamb and not a real puppy.

September 22, 2003
"Fingerprints"

I am really so tired of feeling so lousy and bad all the time. I want to say to myself, "for heaven sakes, get over it; this has been going on long enough!" I feel as though I constantly hit a brick wall. I'm over putting up this fake front that all is well and I'm doing just fine because you know what? I'm not doing fine! I'm not able to fool myself into thinking I'm all right. I'm writing at 6:30 in the morning, which isn't all that early for me, but I've already been up for two hours. The big black cloud is hanging over my head. I have been downstairs going through stacks and stacks of paper. I'm trying to sort through bills and important papers. I find a fairly large stack of papers that is held together with a large spring clip. I see that it is the instructions on how to re-build a MR2 engine that Daniel had made a copy from a CD he had bought. I toss it in the garbage because it is so painful to look at then I quickly grabbed it back out again. The pages are full of black oily fingerprints. I know these are Daniel's fingerprints. They are all over these printed instructions. He obviously had used these papers when he worked on his car in the garage. How do I possibly throw away dirty pages that have his fingerprints all over them? As I am filing away papers I remember the file that Karl had put Daniel's suicide note in. I knew what I was doing and exactly where I was going. It wasn't as if I accidentally stumbled upon the note. I went search-ing for it! I want so desperately to find that missing clue-that missing piece of this great mystery. Why? Why did he do it? Why can't I find the answer to this one question? The question that never leaves me-why? Why can't I find peace with the unknowing. I keep thinking that one day I'll find the answer but in all hon-esty I know I won't.

Yesterday was twenty-nine weeks. I try to find the smallest milestone and the smallest ray of hope. I found such a thing this morning. I don't cry everyday. I'm not sure when I reached this point but I do know it was very recently. I know it was far past his birthday and past the six-month mark. You would have thought I would have remembered the exact day and sent off the fireworks to celebrate but it came and went very quietly without any fanfare. Oh sure, I still cry just like I did this morning when I saw his fingerprints but thank God, and I truly mean thank God, it's not everyday. When I realized I had made it the entire day I almost had a twinge of guilt. Does this mean I'm forgetting him? Is this a healthy sign that I'm moving along in my grieving process? Do I feel guilty that I'm moving on? Is my next step to look forward with anticipation to the time when I can go an entire week without crying? That seems so far in the future that I can't possibly fathom the possibility of no tears for a week.

Chapter 8

Months 8 & 9

"Seeing progress"

___October 2, 2003___
"Hope"

Today is the seventh month anniversary of the death of my son. Who would have ever imagined that I would ever be keeping a journal of my thoughts because I had a child who killed himself? I would have never believed you if this had been told to me seven months and one day ago. It is because of this disbelief that I now believe anything could happen. Things that I used to think would never happen now I find myself thinking it could happen. My trust in people seems shot.

Seven months isn't very long, but I am seeing milestones. Small as they may seem, there is progress. I guess any movement is better than none, no matter how small it may appear. I read back over these pages and see so much sadness and pain especially in the first few weeks. This gives me hope, lots of hope. I feel as though I am healing and moving forward. I can remember a very short time ago that one morning I was looking in the mirror. I was trying so hard to figure out what my reflection meant. I looked in the mirror and saw a reflection that looked ok and normal looking. I kept wondering how that could be. How could I possibly look normal when I knew what I felt like on the inside? My insides felt like jelly and then other times I felt as though I had hundreds and hundreds of sharp knives or razor blades going around inside of me. I would keep looking at my reflection that was staring back at me and think this must be what others see when they look at me. I look ok but I knew I wasn't. There were days I was literally hanging on by a thread. I felt so on edge and the least little thing would or could set me off easily.

I remember a conversation I had with a very dear friend recently. I was having a very casual phone conversation with her. I had called her for what purpose I no longer remember. In talking with her she asked how I was doing. It had been a while since we had last spoken with each other. She is a close friend and I felt I could give her more than the standard pat answer of fine. I said, "I'm ok, not fine, but ok and I still have good days and bad days." She seemed so taken by my answer. Her response was "Really? Do you still have bad days?" I can remember being so taken back by her answer. This conversation took place at about the six-month anniversary. I immediately remembered the morning that I stood at my bathroom mirror and thought my reflection looked ok. I looked ok on the outside but I knew I felt so much pain in the inside. It truly feels as if razor blades are inside of me. I thought this reflection is what she sees and why she would think I'm ok because my outside does look ok. I am so thankful, so very thankful, that these are no longer my hourly feelings.

I still have good days and bad days and I so appreciate the good days. I still wish I had some kind of notice that the blind-sided moments were coming. This morning while I was getting dressed I heard a song that was on an early morning news program. I don't know why the song stung my heart so painfully. The words of the song did not exactly pertain to Daniel as some songs do. They're some songs that will make me cry every time I hear them and it doesn't matter how many times I have already heard them in the past. This song I was listening to this morning had one line about your picture hanging on the wall. I am standing in my bedroom as I hear these words and I turn to the wall where Daniel's picture is hanging. I totally lose it. I actually surprised myself this morning. It had been just a few short days ago since I had last cried. This morning it felt as though the floodgates were opened and all those penned up tears came rushing out. It was as if a pressure valve had been turned to release some built up pressure. I'm thinking perhaps my body liked it better when I cried everyday because the crying this morning was extremely physical and very intense. When I cried everyday it was like a huge pressure release that the human body needed to release. Perhaps crying everyday is better for the body.

October 16, 2003
"Looking for the right therapist"

Today was my regularly scheduled weekly appointment with my therapist. As I wrote in an earlier entry I like going because I enjoy my "safe place" that I can so easily speak about Daniel. I left there today without confirming my next week's appointment and I do not have another appointment scheduled. I feel as though she is no longer taking me to the place that I need to go. I don't know how to describe it but it is a definite feeling of the two of us no longer being in sync. She is all about getting me and keeping me distracted. I feel guilty when I go back and have not yet completed my "to do" list. I mentioned that perhaps I would like to go back to school and she was all over that. I didn't mean I wanted to go back to school the next day. So now I feel guilty if I haven't accomplished her "to do" list. There is not a list I can do right now. My days are still foggy or cloudy. The thought of having to pay attention in a formal classroom does not sound as though I could do it right now in my life. There are lots of areas that I see where this therapist would be excellent. I really do like her and she would be the type of person that I could easily be a friend with. She is the type of person that I could go to lunch with and enjoy her company immensely. I have really been doing a lot of soul searching. I have come to the conclusion that it takes a very special therapist with an enormous amount of knowledge and experience to deal with a client who is dealing with the suicide of a child. Yes, there is an enormous amount of grief but there are so many more issues when it is compounded with suicide. I was thinking this morning that if I had a brain tumor I would not go to a foot doctor. It would not be because the foot doctor is not any good but because I need something more than a foot doctor. I have to take care of me now and seeing that I get matched with the most helpful therapist has got to be a high priority for me. I can now see where people would become very frustrated with how they feel their therapy is working for them and have no desires to continue not realizing you need to research and ask questions until you find the best one for you. If we aren't happy with a doctor we will choose another and that must also be the case with our therapist. I need to find someone who is an expert with grief, trauma and suicide and not necessarily women's issues of low self-esteem or marital problems.

October 28, 2003
"Life is a gift, a priceless gift"

What a glorious and beautiful day it is today. This afternoon Katelynn Elizabeth came into the world. This is Missy and Tim's second child. This morning as I was driving over to the hospital I was overcome with a flood of emotions. I was having so many feelings. I found myself driving down the interstate with utter joy and gratitude. I was beyond happy to be part of the birth experience. There is nothing sweeter or closer to God than being in the room when a precious little newborn makes their appearance in the world. I knew I would soon be looking into the eyes of a special little soul who would be the first niece or nephew who would never meet Daniel. Or would they have met Daniel in the spirit world? I wish I knew if spirits in the same family ever meet as they cross over the veil to either leave the spirit world or return back to the spirit world. I have always hoped they meet one another since we are all family. My father died when I was sixteen years old. My father loved children very much and I was sad that my children never had the experience of having him as a grandfather. He would have been the best. I do hope that my children's paths have somehow crossed with my dad's before they were born just as I hope and wonder if Daniel and Katelynn's spirits have ever crossed. I remember it was only a few days after Daniel died that Missy told me she was pregnant. She was very concerned because of her past history of miscarriages. I remember feeling instantly that this little baby would be fine. The Lord would surely bless us. In the year 2003 we needed desperately to have joy! We needed 2003 to be a year that we would remember a birth date and not just a death date. I never once worried about Missy as I had in the past. I knew from the very moment she told me about this pregnancy that this baby would be perfectly fine.

As I drove to the hospital I was concerned that Missy be comfortable and have an easy delivery. I was so excited to finally meet this special little baby that I had bonded with at the very moment I knew was coming. I was thrilled to see her and hold her in my arms. She is adorable and precious and as I looked at her beautiful little face and those gorgeous blue eyes I felt myself wondering if she and Daniel had shared even a moment together before she was born. Is she now the last one in our family to have seen Daniel? If only she could speak and tell me. Today I also realized once again that life is so precious. Life is a gift, a priceless gift. Just as there is death there is also birth.

November 2, 2003
"Stopping by to check on Mom"

Today is the eighth month anniversary and this is the first time the anniversary has actually fallen on a Sunday. Karl is on a business trip on the other side of the world. He is in Bahrain. I don't like it when he leaves the country because I can't talk to him. I can't even call his cell phone and leave him messages. Even before Daniel died he would travel and leave the country. Karl retired from the Navy after serving for twenty years. We went through four six month deployments, two four month deployments and countless numbers of four and six week exercises. I have had the experience of being separated from my husband but since Daniel has died I have such a hard time being separated from him. I miss him so much and am so anxious for him to get back home. I felt so bad for him when he left for this trip. He was sick with the flu and felt horrible. It has been said that stress can easily bring on an illness. For several weeks now I have known that Karl wasn't doing well. The kids are even making comments about their dad. We all feel he is depressed but we aren't able to bring it up to him. He doesn't want to deal with it or talk about it. I have tried to talk to him about going and getting a prescription for an anti-depressant. Is it pride, denial? Who knows, but we are living with an unhappy person.

Tomorrow is little Ben's 4th birthday. So I am so glad that Laurie is having us all over at her house later today. This is the first Sunday of the month but I am glad we aren't going to be at my house. I have thought about Daniel so much lately. The children seem to be mentioning him a lot also. There are so many times that I feel as though he is right here beside me. Yesterday the feeling was amazingly strong. I was home alone and I walked into the kitchen and said out loud. "What is it? What do you want? I know you are here and there is something you are trying to tell me but I can't figure it out. Help me figure out what it is you want me to know." I can't describe it and I have no idea how it works but I know it's him. I don't see him and I don't hear him but I know as well as I know my name that he is near me. There is a definite void when he isn't around so I have become acutely aware when I do feel his spirit near me. I cannot wait for the day when we will have all the answers and we will know how it all works, I hope I get the answer someday as to how you can absolutely feel the presence of a loved one and yet not see them, hear them or touch them. But I am grateful for the moments when he does "stop by" to check on his mom.

November 15, 2003
"Taking care of family"

When I left my last appointment with my therapist I didn't make another appointment. I am beginning to wonder if that was a mistake. I know it's not a mistake to have not made the appointment with this previous counselor because I really miss my "talking about Daniel" sessions. "Moms" always seem to come in last in the "needs attention" list. One child in particular is in a crisis in trying to deal with Daniel's death. Everything in life comes to a screeching halt and all focus is now directed to this child and this is how it should be in my opinion. There have been a couple of immediate things that have happened because of the directional pull that has now gravitated towards this particular child. In the immediate past there was an enormous amount of grieving that used large amounts of energy and this was directly focused towards the death of Daniel. It is staggering to me the amount of work and energy that is involved in grieving. Circumstances of home will not allow me to stay in the place I have been for weeks and it is strange to be so emotionally charged and it not be about my grief towards Daniel. It is at these times I get angry at Daniel. I get angry that his senseless act has bought so much pain to my surviving children. They did not ask for this nor do they deserve to be so horribly subjected to so much pain. My anger doesn't last long because I quickly realize he too was in a great deal of pain himself. But there is still the mother in me that feels so strongly about not allowing anyone to mess with my kids. This includes Daniel because of what he has caused to his siblings. I want to take the pain from them. I want to shoulder it all so they can escape these painful feelings. Once again old familiar feelings reappear of wanting to fast forward the tape of life. I want to see that the children are going to pull thru this and all will be ok. I hold onto the phrase that time heals all wounds. Even though this wound is very deep and extremely painful I have to believe that time will make it better. No human can stay in this much pain and grieve so heavily and still have any type of a decent life.

Chapter 9

Months 10 + 11

"More anticipation"

November 30, 2003
"Distractions from grieving are blessings"

Sometimes life just happens and that is ok because things work out better than I could have planned it. Thanksgiving is a sweet time of year for us because it is a time for family gatherings and relaxed afternoons over the long weekend to be together and enjoy each other's company. I usually do the majority of the cooking and all the children, the spouses and grandchildren come for the big dinner. We usually get together for a couple of more times during the weekend so the leftovers can be eaten. Plans were in place to have the traditional turkey dinner with all the trimmings. Thanksgiving isn't a holiday that would automatically bring up lots of past Thanksgiving memories of Daniel. Daniel was always home for Thanksgiving and he enjoyed the food but the weekend of football was enjoyed much more. Thanksgiving is a busy holiday for me because I do the shopping and cooking for the majority of the weekend. I was going to be grateful for so many distractions and constantly being on the go. I love it when even the smallest amount of time is diverted from grieving. It is never a long space that there is no grieving and the loss of Daniel never leaves my mind but any distraction is a welcomed relief from the sorrow I feel from Daniel's death. On the Friday before Thanksgiving I discovered by talking to my mother that she was very ill and was bed ridden. This was due to a back injury and she had no recollection of how she hurt her back so badly. I knew I needed to go and check on her. My mom lives in Alabama, so the Wednesday before Thanksgiving we joined the masses on the interstates and drove the 14 hours to my mother's. It was definitely different to be away from home on Thanksgiving. We had the great blessing of being somewhere other than home for the holiday weekend. Amy became very ill with the flu while driving to Alabama. My weekend was consumed with taking care of my mom and Amy. It was a whirlwind trip that zoomed by so quickly. I know we ate a turkey dinner that had been preordered by my mother earlier in November so I did very little cooking. It was a very fast trip and little time was given to think about it being Thanksgiving so that meant very little time to think about this being the first Thanksgiving that Daniel was not with us. This trip became a little blessing in disguise because mom needed me and we took off at the last minute to go be with her.

December 28, 2003
"Going away for Christmas"

Weeks before Christmas it was decided by the family that perhaps it would not be a good idea to stay home for Christmas. I knew the first Christmas with out Daniel was going to be extremely hard for me. I love Christmas and everything that goes with Christmas. In the past I would start decorating Thanksgiving weekend and decorate all over the house. There is always the big tree and smaller trees through out the house. Stockings are hung on the fireplace mantle and splashes of red and green can be seen all over the house. It was in early November that we decided to meet Karl's family in a central location that would be convenient for the five siblings, their families and his mother. It was decided that Asheville, NC would be a good location that would be equal distance for all members. We found a beautiful eight bedroom cabin in the mountains near a beautiful lake. We decided that we would try to get the largest number of people together for at least two nights. There were too many work schedules to work around and there were families with very small children that wanted to be in their own homes for Christmas morning. Christmas this year was on a Thursday. We rented the cabin from the Friday before Christmas to the Friday after Christmas. We knew the majority of the family would be able to come the weekend before Christmas. We found out for only a couple of hundred dollars more we could have the cabin for one week versus four days. When I found out that we could stay in Asheville I was excited because I knew I didn't have to go back home for

Christmas Eve and Christmas Day. I could actually be absent from my house on this very first crucial Christmas. I knew and understood completely that the married children would be heading back to their homes to celebrate Christmas morning at their own houses but I felt as though I could not spend Christmas at my home this year.

I had told my children that I couldn't decorate the house in its usual splendor this year. It was too painful. I had been told by several that there was no right or wrong way to celebrate the holidays when you have lost a loved one. Whatever it takes to get you through it is the correct way. I felt for the three children still living here at home but there was no way I could look at all those decorations. I knew my limitations and this Christmas was so painful. I became teary eyed walking through the stores and seeing the Christmas decorations. I couldn't listen to Christmas carols at home or on the radio. Everything was such a vivid and visual reminder that Daniel wasn't going to be with us this Christmas season. In years past I lived with anticipation and excitement for months in advance that Christmas was coming. I loved the season of giving and especially to my family. I would shop early with great thoughts and preparations in every gift. I loved to see their faces as I saw their excitement with gifts I had bought them. I loved to give them gifts that I had overheard them speak of that they would like to have or would enjoy having. My gifts were not gifts that were given just for the task of fulfilling an assignment of giving. I gave lots of thought and time in my gift giving. I couldn't believe it. It was the middle of December and I hadn't bought any gifts this year nor had any decorations in the house. My birthday is December 9th and I decided to treat myself and I would buy something I had always wanted for Christmas decorations. A large department store was having a 50% off sale on their little Christmas villages. I bought four pieces that were either houses, a chapel or a store. I bought people and several other small pieces that would accent the village scene at Christmas time. I brought it home and put it on the mantle where the Christmas stockings would have normally hung. I also found a collection of six glass butterfly tree ornaments and one of the butterflies was yellow. I bought a very small tree to put on the library table in the living room and decorated it with the butterfly ornaments and a single string of white lights. This is all the decorations that went up this year. One thing about it; the tear down and clean up will be a breeze.

In buying the small tree I also bought an even smaller tree that was purchased for Daniel's marker. The little tree was already weighted down and covered in Christmas material at the bottom. I knew it would sit very well on the marker. I also bought red silk poinsettias for the vase. On my way home from the store I stopped by the cemetery. I was surprised that I was overcome by so much emotional grief as I placed the little Christmas tree on the marker. I go often to his marker to put fresh flowers or change the silk arrangements in the vase. It has become an act of love and remembrance and I no longer cry every time I go to the cemetery. So I was a little taken back when the tears came so easily. I know exactly what the tears mean. I am so sad that I have bought a small Christmas tree and silk flowers for my son's grave. I want to buy his favorite cologne, his favorite subscription to the car magazine that he loves the most. I want to know that he is going to be around to read all twelve issues of the latest car magazine. Oh God, more than anything I want him home for Christmas. I don't want to be standing over his grave. Daniel has been with me for the last nineteen Christmases. I do not want to spend the first of many Christmases to come without Daniel.

I made it through Christmas and the holidays mainly because I wasn't at home. We met Karl's family in Asheville, NC at the large house in the mountains. The majority of the group met there on Friday night before Christmas that was on Thursday this year. Family members trickled in as their schedules allowed. On Saturday night everyone was there and we had thirty eight family members in eight different bedrooms, two living room couches and children's sleeping bags in so many different corners through out the house. I mention the large crowd because it felt so strange to wake up Sunday morning and feel so alone, sad and depressed and yet the house I am in is bursting at the seams with thirty eight people. On that morning I took a long two hour walk by myself and shed lots and lots of tears. It was on this walk and one other time on Christmas night that I cried long and hard. Tears constantly bubbled up to the surface but I was able to force them back down since there was so much going on around me and I was easily distracted. I loved my walk. I was in the most beautiful place and I loved the beautiful scenery. This community is built around a lake. There is a road that goes around the lake. It took several miles to complete the circle around the lake and the views were gorgeous. A snow storm had come through on Friday night as we arrived. The roads were now cleared but snow still covered everything. I felt as though I was walking in a scene from an Irving and Ives Christmas card.

Daniel has a male cousin that is only a few weeks younger than Daniel. These two were inseparable when they got together. I have always wished that our families had spent more time together because it was so obvious these two boy cousins had a great love for each other and thoroughly loved being in each other's company. He came for Daniel's funeral and I had not seen him since. I was saddened now to see him without his buddy. He looked so lost to be at a family gathering and not have his trusty side kick. At all family reunions in the past where there was one you could easily find the other. I made a couple of attempts to talk to him and see how he was doing but I felt very limited in my ability to talk with him. I wanted Daniel to be there for him just as much as he wanted Daniel to be there. I was so afraid that I was going to make it so much worse for him by breaking down and crying in front of him. I hurt so badly for him that I could never get very far in the conversation. I always backed down and moved on when I felt the opening of the flood gates. I wish now I had talked more to him. I would have loved to have him tell me his favorite Daniel stories. Now I think how silly it was to be afraid to cry in front of him. He knows how much I love Daniel and I know how much he loves Daniel. Tears shared between us would have been perfectly ok.

Several months ago I decided to make small scrapbooks for the children with pictures of Daniel. After going through all the pictures I was surprised at how many pictures I found of the children that were one on one with Daniel. They will be perfect for their individual scrapbooks. Joseph had asked if I would please get together some pictures of Daniel that he could take back to school with him after the Christmas holidays. I decided I would do Joseph's book first. I had brought all "my stuff" to North Carolina because I needed to finish the last three pages. Karl's brother and his family left to go home early in the evening on Christmas night. It was now just me, Karl, Joseph, Jenny, Amy and Matt at the cabin. We had a nice dinner and everyone realized how tired they were from a week of constantly being on the go and staying up late every night. It was after eleven and everyone had decided to go to bed. I took this opportunity of a very quiet house to finish Joseph's book. I was enjoying the time by myself and especially glad to finally finish the book for Joseph so he could take it home with him. Check out time for the cabin was twelve noon the next day. It was during this quiet, peaceful time that I became acutely aware that Daniel was with me. I quickly teared up not because of sadness but I had such a confirmation that I knew without a shadow of a doubt that he was there in the room with me. I wish I could explain it or make sense of it myself. There is no way to explain it but it is as real as anything else that I know for sure in this world. I don't know why he comes around when he does. A few things I do know for sure. This never happens when I call out to him or request a visit from him. It is always when I least expect it and I am in a still quite place. I remember stopping what I was doing and speaking out loud to him. I said, "You are here, aren't you? I think you have come to wish your mama a Merry Christmas and let me know you've missed being with us all day." Immediately, and I do mean immediately it came so strong, "Yes Mom, yes, I am here." I started to cry but said the dumbest thing. I said, "Dan, just a minute I can't go there just yet.." I made what now seems like such a dumb comment because I was so afraid if I totally gave into the moment I would fall apart. I was worried about putting the finishing touches on the last page of the book. I actually said you have to wait one minute just as I would have done in the past when he was alive. How many times are mothers interrupted in a single day by their children and we tell them just a minute we will be right there? So I quickly finished the last page and cleaned up my belongings from the dining room table. I went and sat on the living room sofa but it was too late. I never felt him. I knew for sure he was no longer there and had moved on to wherever he goes and does whatever he does. I learned a very important lesson from all this. Daniel can never be summoned by my mere request. I feel his spirit near me when I least expect it and there is no denying that it is him. I question now if I had stopped at that very moment if I would have felt anything else from him. I doubt that I would have. That was my gift however brief it was to me. There is no doubt in my mind that Daniel knows how much his mother loves Christmas and I would certainly be missing him tremendously on Christmas. The entire day I had never stopped long enough to be still and find peace and quite until late in the evening. It was almost at the first opportunity he had he took advantage of that time. Even though I was not able to see him with my physical eyes I felt his spirit. It spoke volumes to me in the sense that he is very aware of my earthly existence and he knew how much I missed having him with me on Christmas Day.

Even though I can not summon him at will for my convenience I have to say that I am glad it works that way. At times I think how nice that would be if it did work that way but I know I would totally abuse the heck out of that deal. So when he does come it is such a feeling of love and happiness and I take it for being the gift that it is. It is such a sweet gift and it is never expected. This reminds me of something that happened in November. It is strange because I can at times feel him constantly with me and yet there is not a real cut and dry message. Yet, I have this incredible, overwhelming feeling of his presence. The first of November I couldn't go and do anything without feeling him constantly. It was an overpowering feeling that would not go away. I distinctly remember one day coming into the house and I was the only one at home. When I got into the kitchen I just let out in this loud voice "what do you want? I know you are here and there must be something that is really important that you are trying to tell me. I know you are here. I have felt you for days. I know you are here for a purpose and I can't figure it out. You have got to help me because I don't have a clue. I don't know what you are trying to tell me. Help me find the answer." Now I know yelling or speaking in a loud voice made no difference but I felt so frustrated. I had felt this feeling for days and days and I was sure he was there to help but help with what I did not know. The interesting part of this story is only a couple of days later something very significant happened to one of the children still living at home. It was a crisis and needed our immediate attention. I know now Daniel had to have been aware of it from the beginning and was trying to get the message to us the parents that this particular sibling needed our attention. Once again it is more affirmation that Daniel is very much aware of us and knows what goes on around us. I look forward to one day knowing how all this works. It will be interesting to see how much we can see and know what goes on in our family lives even after we have left them in their earthly state.

January 29, 2004
"Staying busy helps"

New Year's Day and Eve ended up being worse holidays than Christmas. When the clock struck twelve midnight I was overcome from such sadness that I had to go off by myself for a few minutes to cry. It is so painful to think that this will be a full and complete year without Daniel. Not one day will I be with Daniel in 2004 and how many more years will I go before I see him again. I am sure now that I made it through Christmas and the holidays because I wasn't at home. I certainly had my moments that were very painful and very difficult to get through but I am glad I wasn't at home. I can remember my early days in therapy and I voiced my concern about how I would spend the first Christmas without Daniel. Her advice was very helpful and I took lots of time pondering her advice. She told me there is no answer that will tell me how to spend my holidays. There simply is no correct answer because I have to do whatever it takes for me to get through it. Whatever Karl and I agree upon is the correct answer. The other family members must understand how difficult this Christmas will be for us and be willing to support our decision on this very painful issue. I am grateful that Karl also wanted to be away from home over the holidays. I wonder what happens when couples cannot agree on how to spend those first crucial holidays and anniversaries after the death of their child.

Something has begun to take place that is very uncomfortable and yet I don't have the energy to combat it or even deal with it. I am spending an enormous amount of time in bed. I manage to get the children out the door to school but back to bed I go. At the time of Daniel's death I was extremely busy and engaged in multi-tasking all day long. I was very involved in volunteer work for my church. I was a Relief Society President. Many hours a day is devoted to volunteering my time and services to women of different ages but mainly the elderly who no longer drive or have family living near by who would be able to assist in their needs. I only bring this up for one reason. After Daniel died I did not relinquish duties as Relief Society President. I can remember being out of circulation for two or three weeks immediately following Daniel's death but then I went right back to work. I look back now and wonder how I did it. I have an old planner that is full of appointments that I made and kept but this seems to be my only memory of the things I did on a daily basis. I am very grateful that I was able to stay so busy and very distracted. I had little time to think because I was always taking care of someone else whether it was my children or women of my church. It was mid November when I realized my family had to be my first priority and I had to give my attention totally to them and in particular one daughter who was struggling a lot. I was released from my position as Relief Society President in mid December. It was after the holidays that I realized how much empty time I had on my hands and I started to think for the first time since his death and I didn't like it! I first blamed staying at home and in my bed on the cold weather, saying it was too cold to go outside and do anything. It is just too darn easy to climb back in that bed everyday. So that is where the majority of my time is spent, sleeping fifteen to eighteen hours a day which leaves little time to do any thing else, especially writing in the journal.

Chapter 10

One year - Month 15

"The anniversary, again the anticipation is worse than the event"

February 17, 2004
"Parents Group"

It feels as though there are lots of gaps and missing spaces as I look back over these last few entries. I find it hard to write now. I am sure the upcoming one year anniversary is playing a vital role in all these feelings that are going around in my head. In the month following Daniel's death, Karl and I received a newsletter from a parents group whose purpose is to help grieving parents. This group holds monthly meetings on the fourth Monday evening of each month in a church not very far from our house. Karl and I have decided to attend in search of answers to our questions. We have no idea what to do on the first anniversary date of our child who has died. Perhaps there will be other parents who can enlighten us on this dilemma we are facing. I certainly do not want to ignore this date nor do I want to look as though we are having some sort of celebration in order that the day not be ignored.

February 24, 2004
"Empathy"

Last night was such a success as far as getting the information we needed and also the group was so kind, sweet and understanding. I am so glad we went. It was hard at first. I would be lying if I said it was all a walk in the park. In fact it was a long walk from the parking lot to the building. Once we got inside we were greeted by very kind people and people who truly understood. We sat in a circle and gave our names and told what brought us to the parents group. There were tears because I was finally able to tell someone about the grief I felt as a mother of a child who had died. I knew for a fact everyone in that room knew exactly how I felt and knew from first hand experience what I was feeling at that moment. I knew I had finally met people who said they were sorry and understood what I was feeling. I knew they were speaking from their own pain and experiences of losing a child.

March 2, 2004
"The anniversary, a time for favorite memories"

One year ago today Daniel took his own life! I am still full of the same question: why? I have not yet begun to accept the fact that Daniel chose suicide. I will never accept full acceptance of that but I am beginning to accept that I will never know why in this lifetime. I have also come to realize that the anticipation of the day is so much worse than the actual day. This seems to be occurring a lot. I can remember dreading the first month anniversary and also his birthday with a great deal of fear. I faced the holidays and then the first year anniversary of his death with lots of fear because I did not know what the day would bring.

Karl and I woke up this morning and realized it really wasn't any different than any other day. Daniel still wasn't here, we still missed him as much as ever and the pain was still there. I had been so concerned as to how I would spend the day that I wasn't really sure what I wanted to do during the day. I knew we had made plans for the evening. I didn't want to celebrate it or overly emphasize the day as being the day of Daniel's death. But I knew I did not want to treat it as though it were just another day in the week. I wanted to acknowledge it for what it was but concentrate more on the living Daniel. The great memories I had of Daniel when he was alive and not his dying was how I wanted to spend the day.

Amy had asked if she could stay home from school and yet Matt wanted to go to school. Karl, Jenny, Amy and I went out to lunch. After lunch Karl and I went to the cemetery for what reason I am not sure. It's like one of those thousands of things that we don't have a clue about what to do. It just seemed like the kind of thing one would do on the death anniversary. I had already gone the day before and put beautiful spring flowers on the marker and removed the Valentine arrangement. It was an extremely windy day, very cloudy, gray and a chilly day. It wasn't a pleasant place to be because we had to stand outside. We both looked down at the marker and we cannot believe our child's body is in the ground at that spot where we stood. I mean you talk about total denial and I give you a great example of denial. It cannot be possible that I have a child that is dead. I look at that marker, see Daniel's full name and still can't believe its Daniel's grave-that he is actually dead and buried there. We were there about 2:30 in the afternoon. It was not planned that way at all. It was never intended for us to be at the cemetery at the exact same time one year ago earlier that we had first found Daniel. I cannot believe what all we have been through in 365 days.

In January I had asked all the children, the older children's spouses and the two grandmothers to please write down their favorite Daniel memory. I also included a couple of Daniel's closest friends to please do the same. They could mail it or email it to me. I wanted to put these favorite stories in a booklet and make copies for all of us. It was after the parent's group meeting that we decided to alter the plans slightly. One parent had told us that on his daughter's anniversary of her death the family and her friends gathered together to share their favorite stories of her. Since I had already asked family members to write down their favorite Daniel memory, we decided to have everyone come over that evening and read their story out loud. Joe, Nana, and grandmamma had sent their stories by email. Family members read their stories since they could not be with us. It turned out to be a very good evening. We had laughter and tears and we were able to share some wonderful and sweet memories. I am so glad we did what we did. I feel as though we all gained from the experience and it felt good to laugh about Daniel and remember such sweet, nice things about a great kid and he was a great kid.

It is now late in the evening as I write and I have had time for reflection of the day. A couple of things come to mind immediately. First of all, it has not been a bad day. The day I have been dreading for probably ten or eleven months was far worse in my mind of what I thought it would be like than the actual day. I still have the same thoughts at the end of this day as I did when I first opened my eyes this morning. The pain is still there and it is not any different just because it is the anniversary. I still miss him terribly and wish he was here with me. Those feelings make no difference what day it is. Secondly, I would have to say how touched I am with people who have remembered what day this is. Tonight Tim was telling us that he went to the cemetery around eleven this morning. He saw where someone had left a card. He didn't look to see who it was from. The wind had definitely blown it away by the time we got to the cemetery. Later in the day a friend of Amy's had called the house to get directions to the cemetery. She wanted to take flowers and leave them on his marker. In the mail today we got two cards from friends who were aware of the anniversary date and were letting us know they were thinking about us. One card had the sweetest message that was sent with lots of love. It made Karl and I feel so good that he had remembered March 2nd and he remembered us. But you know why it also made us feel so good? Someone still remembered Daniel and he is not forgotten. As a mom I worry greatly about Daniel's memory. As a mom I know I'll never forget so I don't want others to forget either. I worry that after me and Karl pass on who will still care and want to keep Daniel's memory alive.

March 5, 2004
"The Comforter"

The one year anniversary of Daniel's death comes with mixed emotions. It has now been 368 days without Daniel being physically with me. I can no longer remember or visualize what Daniel was doing or may have been doing one year ago. It's with a bitter sweet thought that I can no longer say one year ago today Daniel was … I am grateful for coming through the most horrible, horrific year of my entire life. I won't say made it. I sure don't feel as though I've made it. I remember going to bed near midnight on the one year anniversary of Daniel's death. I snuggled up close to Karl and whispered, "We did it. We survived the first year." That's about how I actually feel. I survived. I have no idea how I did it. I do know with absolute certainty that I didn't do it by myself. My Heavenly Father was fore most the reason I made it thus far and the love of family and friends have been so needed and appreciated.

I look back at some of the things I did last year and I truly have no idea how I did any of it. There is no doubt that my faith and beliefs made an enormous difference in how I handled things. I know I reached down deep and tapped into an inner strength that I never knew existed. I know my spiritual self was continually fed and nourished on a daily basis by a power far greater than I. There is no way I would have ever begun to have made it thus far without the help of God and the Holy Comforter. I wish I had the literary skills to write what I actually felt on countless days. I don't know if there are words that could describe the miracle I experienced. There were so many days that I found myself in a heap somewhere sobbing my eyes out with no desire to move on. Each and every time it was the Comforter that always was there to gather me up and bring me comfort and assurance. In my deepest darkest days I sometimes wondered how I would exist another five minutes without my Daniel. Journal writing became very difficult and writing took a very low spot on the priority list. But I wish I could put into words the magnificent power of the Comforter. When total hopelessness, despair and total grief came over me the Comforter would come. It felt as though I was being scooped up from this incredible mess, cradled in his arms and told I was not alone.

As the one year anniversary approached I became very sad and grief stricken. Karl said he felt the same way. These feelings felt scary because they felt so intense. We both agreed that one year ago in the beginning our feelings were horrible and unimaginable. Then things seemed to ease up around the six to eight month time period. But now that we are at the one year mark it feels as though it is a fast downhill spiral. All doubts and fears seem to be intense and magnified. It almost feels as though we are back in the beginning of the grieving process. I am so glad that I have this journal to look back on because I can see there were days that weren't as bad as these days that I am experiencing now. So now I do know it is possible to have better days than what I am feeling currently. In this journey of grief I have learned that there will be peaks and valleys along the way.

April 5, 2004
"I want to go somewhere where there isn't any more pain"

Everything is very difficult for me right now. I have decided to go back into therapy. I have found someone who I like a lot. She is very experienced in grief counseling and deaths dealing with trauma. I need a place to go and talk and share all these feelings I am experiencing. I am beginning to worry. How will I ever have my life back? I have begun to doubt every thing I have felt in the past year. I now question what it was that I felt in the past year. What if everything is wrong and all these feelings were just made up feelings and beliefs on my part. What if all I have experienced in the last year is nothing more than false hope. All this time I have been making myself believe that I had Daniel forever because that is the only way I could ever survive. There is no way I could ever accept anything else. I have forced myself to believe those things only to survive. Now that a year has gone by what if reality is finally settling in and the real truth is I have lost Daniel. I tell myself over and over hundreds of times that the "what ifs" and the question of "why" will destroy you. I once read the person who kills himself will die once and the loved ones left behind will die a thousand times or more. I believe it! The self doubt will destroy you and that's what is happening to me. It has come on with a vengeance since the New Year. I hate the fact that I will spend every day of 2004 without Daniel and countless more years. All I know is I feel horrible but I do feel good about my decision to go to another therapist. There are certainly good therapists and bad ones. Even the bad ones may not be necessarily bad but their strengths may not be in grief counseling. I have definitely learned how critical it is to find the right therapist for myself. I was very fortunate and found her through the parents group. What a great avenue to use; go to the source where death and grief is the main focus.

I had an experience a few weeks ago that was an eye opening experience that showed me I could no longer do this by myself. Every since Christmas I thought of calling my family and friends so many times but they are all so busy and I didn't want to put this on them. That's another important reason for a therapist. You won't burn out your family and friends if you have a therapist. I felt as though family and friends had had more than enough of me.

A few weeks ago I seemed to be paralyzed with fear. The only relief I got was from sleeping. I was functioning at the very, very bare minimum. I didn't want to draw attention to myself so I said nothing. What a joke that must have been, who wouldn't have noticed. I slept all the time and had no desires to do anything or be with anyone. I felt totally numb and dead inside. My biggest fear was not knowing if Daniel was ok or not knowing where he was. This fear gripped me to the point that I was very fearful of what I was thinking. So much so that I knew I had to tell Karl. This was truly a very dark time for me. A time that I am very grateful is over. I never wanted to die in that I wanted to kill myself. It was not as if I were in so much pain that I could no longer go on living. But I had to know if Daniel was ok. I was the mom and all moms know where their children are and how they are doing. I had to know and I could only figure out one way to find this out. I am sure there will be those who will read this and feel sure that I am having suicidal thoughts but I'm not so sure they were. First of all I had no plans or means to carry this out. All I knew was I had to get to Daniel to make sure he was ok but I had no idea how I was going to make this happen. There was one part that had me concerned and that's why I knew I had to tell Karl. I had justi-fied in my mind that it was ok to go to Daniel and find out for myself if he was ok. All would understand that as a mom I had to go find Daniel. I had also justi-fied that every one would be ok without me except Matt. I couldn't allow myself to think of Matt without a mom. He is only twelve years old and still needed a mom. I could never allow myself to completely come to grips with this totally irrational and insane decision thinking process. Matt needed me and I had to stay for him. So I would never allow myself to think beyond that point.

I can remember one particular Tuesday several weeks ago. I lay in bed and I was crying and crying. I did the motherly duty of getting children off to school earlier that morning but it was quickly back in bed after they left. It was around noontime and I couldn't lay there another moment or cry another tear. I decided to go to my mom's house. I knew I had to get away. I desperately needed a place to go that was a change. I became focused and task oriented. I put a load of clothes in the washer and went and got a suitcase from the attic. As I passed the phone I called Karl to tell him of my plans. I had totally fooled myself and made myself believe I was in complete control and I was until I heard his voice on the other end of the phone. I couldn't speak. I started to cry and attempted to get out that I was going to my mom's. He asked if he needed to come home. I told him I wasn't sure because I didn't even know what I needed. I had no idea what anybody could do for me because I didn't know what I needed or what to do for myself. He said he would be right there and he was home from his office in fifteen minutes. I don't want to know how fast he drove. I do remember feeling relieved that he was coming home. When he got home I was upstairs packing. He asked that if I had not been able to get him when I did would I have still left without seeing him to say goodbye. I didn't know. I had no feelings inside, just numb. I asked if he wanted to go with me and he asked where? I remember painfully getting the words out, "Somewhere where it doesn't hurt anymore, somewhere where there isn't any more pain." I broke down beside him on the bed. I told him I couldn't stand not knowing where Daniel was and knowing if he was ok. Karl told me we had to fall back on where we had been before in our faith. We had to rely now more than ever on our faith. This would be our true test of faith, believing in what cannot be seen. I knew he was right but I just wanted the pain to end. I wanted to once again feel a moment of peace. So I just blurted out let's go the temple. The only place I knew where I had even a chance of finding peace. Karl said, "Now?" and I said, "Yes." We both got up and put on church clothes and headed for the temple at 2:00 in the afternoon. It is a three and a half to four hour drive. We made it in time for the 5:30 session. As I sat in the temple I felt that peace that I was longing for! I may have been in the temple for two hours but it was worth every minute I was there to feel that peace. Nowhere on earth can it be found as it is in the temple. Unless you experience it you can never explain it. People would think you are out of your ever loving mind to drive 3 and a half hours one way in the Washington D.C. traffic to only stay two hours and then turn around for another 3 and a half hours to drive back home. Unless you experience the peace in the temple you will never understand the why, the reason I was compelled and driven to go that afternoon in search of peace that I knew could be found in the temple. My testimony was fed and I received a much needed spiritual shot, a great boost to my spiritual well being. I walked away from there knowing I hadn't been wrong in the past with the spiritual feelings and experiences I have had concerning Daniel. I left there once again feeling that Daniel is fine and I knew where he was. Faith truly is believing in what you can't see. As we drove home I had so many thoughts and feelings of gratitude. First of all I am so grateful that Karl loves me so much that he stopped everything he was doing to come and be with me. I know that wasn't easy because he had a lot going on that day and he had to re-arrange several things to make it happen for him to leave the office and come home to me. I am so grateful for temples. Nowhere on earth would I have ever been able to find the peace that I found that night. I am also grateful that I have a current temple recommend and so does Karl. As I drove home feeling so much better with a new sense of comfort and peace; I thought how horrible it would have been to desperately want to go to the temple and not be able to attend because I didn't hold a current temple recommend. Then I thought how grateful I am that Karl also holds a current temple recommend. How sad it would have been if he had not been able to go with me. I am most grateful to Heavenly Father for once again being there for me and letting me know He truly knows me and knows of my needs.

Chapter 11

Months 16 + 17

"Good Therapy"

May 31, 2004
"The Black Jacket"

It's Monday, Memorial Day. I suppose if my journal entries were titled; today's entry would be titled "The Black Jacket". The Christmas before Daniel died I bought him a black jacket. He had seen the jacket at a store and fell in love with the jacket instantly. He came home and immediately told me about the jacket. He was actually very interested in my opinion about the jacket because he wanted to know if he would be able to wear this jacket on his mission on planning days. I agreed to go with him and look at the jacket. It was a great jacket, perfect in every way. It was solid black with no logos or writings. It was lined with a heavy fleece lining for warmth and it also had a water repellent material on the outside. It would be great for all types of weather. I thought it would be great for a missionary who would be outside a great deal of his time. So of course I bought the jacket and I had a sweet, sweet picture in my mind of my future missionary wearing this black jacket. From the first afternoon I bought that jacket he wore it everyday. He loved it! And I loved seeing him wear it because he loved it so much.

On the Sunday evening that Daniel died I saw that black jacket lying on the breakfast nook table. Several times through out the day I saw this black heap of material on the table. I walked up to the table and I remember so vividly my legs shaking, and feeling my knees bend as if they were about to give way. I quickly turned around and found Karl in our bedroom. I asked that he please go and get the black jacket and put it away out of my sight. I knew there was no way I could possibly lift that jacket up off the table. I was certain Daniel had taken it off the night before and just tossed it on the table as he went upstairs to his room. This would have been the exact same routine he had done many times before since acquiring the jacket. Karl came back to tell me that it wasn't the black jacket but a pair of someone's black pants. He did find the jacket in Daniel's room and brought it upstairs and hung it in the farthest back corner of our closet. I knew I would really have to go searching if I wanted that jacket. I also realized that "the black jacket" had an enormous emotional hold on me. Since his death I have often thought of that black jacket a number of times and wished I had the courage to go and wrap myself in it. I could never get past the "thinking about it" stage before the tears would flow like water and I would crumble. I sometimes surprised myself and perhaps even scared myself a little on how much of an emotional hold I had allowed myself to get concerning the black jacket. I was afraid I would not be able to physically stand the pain that I knew I would feel if I held that jacket in my arms. Whenever Daniel showered and went out he always wore his favorite cologne. I knew that jacket would smell like Daniel and I knew I couldn't stand one more undeniable fact that Daniel was gone. I truly felt as though my body would not stand such pain if I smelled Daniel in that jacket.

During my counseling session last week my grief counselor began to explain to me about something called a linking object. She wanted me to think about what my object might be and bring it in next week. She said everyone has at least one object that links yourself to your deceased loved one. As she described this concept about a linking object I knew immediately what my linking object was to Daniel. I told her I knew for sure that mine was Daniel's black jacket but there was no way I could remove it from the closet and bring it next week because I wouldn't be able to go and get it. She suggested that perhaps I just look at it. I could bring it out of the back of the closet and place it in a place that I could see it. Actually what we were doing was addressing the issue of the linking object in different stages and times. I told her that I thought I could do that, look at it but I was not yet ready to hold it.

Last Friday our family went to the beach. I got a bad sunburn on my face. I couldn't believe how badly I burned even though I had used lots of sun block. It must have been out of date. On Sunday morning my face was swollen and I was having difficulty seeing out of my swollen eyes. I decided to stay home from church and place cold compresses on my face and eyes. I was the only one home that morning. I had gone into the closet and for some odd reason I immediately remembered the black jacket. I remembered my agreement to at least pull it out from the very back and place it somewhere so I could see it. I did take the jacket from the back and was ready to place it on a hook that was in plain view. Instead of placing the jacket on the brass hook, I removed the jacket from the hanger. I immediately took the jacket and caressed the jacket up against my face. I then left the closet and went to lay on my bed with the jacket. I held that jacket so tightly and cuddled it as though it were a baby in a blanket. I cried and cried because it was as though all the flood gates were opened and months and months of fear, and emotional ties to that black jacket were suddenly released in one brief moment as I deeply caressed the black jacket. And yes, it smelled like Daniel just as I knew it would. My heart was breaking but I knew a major hurdle had just been crossed.

Let me tell you that black jacket was becoming a huge monster. It was taking on a life of its own. The longer it stayed in the back of that closet the bigger it was becoming and the more fear I had about facing it. My fear of facing that jacket was far bigger than the actual encounter with the jacket on that Sunday morning. I am so happy I have dealt with that jacket and it is no longer sitting in my closet with so much fear attached to it. Yes, it was hard to smell that all too familiar smell of Daniel's cologne but the fear of it always hanging over my head was scarier. The fear and anticipation of touching the jacket that I had on a daily basis was so much worse than actually facing the jacket. The black jacket still remains my linking object and it may remain my linking object for a very long time. But that's ok with me. Today the jacket hangs on the brass hook and I see it every time I open my closet door. I now like looking at the jacket which is amazing to me when I consider how much fear was attached to that jacket a very short time ago. There are even days now that I visualize myself wearing that jacket. Daniel would like that because he knew the pride I felt when I saw him wear it because he liked it so much. He would be proud of me now for making huge courageous steps in this so called journey of grief.

July 22, 2004
"A letter to Daniel"

In my counseling session this afternoon it was recommended that I write a letter to Daniel. I could think of no better place to write such a letter than in my journal.

Dear Daniel,

If only it were so simple to write you a letter, seal it and mail it and know you would receive it. I would go to the ends of this earth if I thought there was even a slight chance that your physical eyes would fall on this page. I would spend the rest of my life searching for you if I thought I had the chance to see you and hold you again.

Next week will be seventeen months since I last saw you and beheld the beauty of your body and spirit. Even as I write that simple sentence it makes me so sad to realize that there will come a day when I say you have been dead for seventeen years and not a mere seventeen months. Time and distance away from you give me so much pain because I grieve so much for you. I can hardly stand it, you have been gone nearly a year and a half. It seems so long ago that I gazed into your sweet face and became captivated by that adorable smile that you are so well known for showing. You always did know how to melt your mother's heart with that one of a kind smile that so easily turned into a grin. It is so unbelievable to me that I will spend the rest of my life with your absence.

If you stood before me this very day I know I would tell you the same things that I feel in my heart today. I am sure I would hug you and squeeze you tightly before I ever said a word. I would cherish that moment so much that I would hold on so tightly and would hesitate and prolong ever letting go of you. There is no doubt that the first words out of my mouth would be, "I love you." I know now I never said it enough to you. Sure, I said it to you when you were alive but how do you ever tell someone that you love them enough times?

I want you to know that I have felt you near me. I know you see me and are aware of my earthly existence. For that I am eternally grateful. I only wish it were more of a two way communication process. I have read that when our loved ones leave us that they love us even more because they now know so much more and are aware of so much more. You and I had a special and wonderful mother and son relationship. I can't imagine how we could love each other more but I guess that's heaven. I want you to know that I grieve so hard for you and feel so sad because I miss you so much. There is comfort in knowing where you are and the great work that I know you are doing. I have never doubted where you are nor have I ever been angry with God. My pain is because I want to see you, hug you and tell you how much I love you.

Do you have any idea how I long to be sitting on my bed and literally see you bounce up the stairs 3 or 4 stairs at a time? You would be in such a hurry to find me so you could tell me something. I want dirty finger prints on the tops of all my door facings. Now why do you suppose that you could never go through a door without touching the top of the door? I want rolls of paper towel to be gone in one or two days because you could never just tear off one. With your strength and you always being in a hurry you would jerk the roll so hard that several paper towels would come off in your hand each time you grabbed just one. I want to buy a gallon of milk each day because you ate cereal all the time as a snack. I want there to be no bowls in the cabinet because they are still in your room and you just haven't gotten around to bringing them all downstairs to the kitchen. I want to lie in my bed late at night and listen out for your car turning the corner and hearing the front door open and now knowing that I could fall asleep because you are safely home. I want to stand at the window without you ever knowing that I am watching you playing basketball, skate boarding in the court or kicking a soccer ball over and over a countless number of times. I would stare as a thin piece of clear glass separated us with such awe and wonderment. How was it possible that anyone could get a human body to do the things that you considered simple and routine? Of all the things that I wish for the most I would have to say it would be one last chance to be with you the night before you died. If I had gone and sat in your room would you have told me how sad you were that she was breaking up with you? Would you have listened if I told you that there would be another girl someday who would love you even more and love you for what you truly were? I want to know and I want to believe so desperately that it would have made a difference if I had been there for you to talk to. Suicide is such a lonely, lonely act and yet I hate you died alone.

It is very important to me that you know I do not have any anger towards you. I forgive you completely. I know in my heart that you never intended to hurt us. I feel sure if you had been allowed to see the aftermath that you would have never gone through with it. I also know it will never be the same and I will never get over this. I am learning to cope with things and deal with things that I never thought I could have done. People ask how I am and I tell them fine but you must know I will never be fine. The day will come that I will be full of joy and happiness and this will be when I see you again and know for sure you are indeed alright and happy. You must know what a struggle this is for me to be happy but I have no choice. I must go on for my living children. They deserve and need a mother who loves life and lives each day to the fullest. It is great to be alive with my dear and special loved ones.

I will be expanding my life into new frontiers. It is not an area that I have been in before nor is it a place that I would chose to be in. But you know life is full of bumps in the road and even detours. My life is taking a new direction due to my tragic loss because of your death. I am now requesting your help. Stay with me and guide me in the direction that I need to go. I want to help another mother or father who may be experiencing the horrible pain and grief that a parent suffers when a child dies. If such a tragedy should happen to them I want them to know there is a place where they can turn and find help. It is my hope that it will be from the pages of my journal that will someday be a book. I want this parent to know what they are feeling is pure raw grief in its most primitive form. I want them to know that they are not going crazy, others have felt the same way and he or she is not alone and there are those who are willing to help. This is where I summon your help. Daniel, my ears are open, my eyes are open but more importantly my heart and soul and spirit are open. My spirit is so willing to serve and I know we can do this together. Please help me find the people who can bring to pass my desires of my heart. Open doors for me that may have been shut or guide me to places and people that I may not have known about. We can do this, I know we can. I love you with all my heart and until we meet again you and I will go forth and do great things. I love you so much, Mom.

Chapter 12

Months 18-23

"Signs and feelings"

August 14, 2004
"The yellow butterfly"

There are a few entries that I question if I want to see on a printed page. I have never been ashamed or embarrassed by my thoughts or feelings but I do wonder if anyone were to ever see this what they would think. This entry deals with something that has been going on for a long time. At first I kind of ignored it thinking it was mere coincidence but after today I realized it is far more than just a coincidence.

I have never looked for a sign or signs to know if Daniel was still around. I have never needed any type of material sign that Daniel is near because I have always felt him on numerous occasions. I have never needed a material object because the feelings I have are so real and I have known he was near. But there is one thing that keeps appearing and I must mention it because it is very real and tangible. My object is a yellow butterfly. No, I do not believe that Daniel has taken on the ability to be inside a yellow butterfly nor do I believe that these appearances are all from the same butterfly.

It all began over a year ago. I do not have the exact date because at the time it didn't seem as though it should be something that would need to be noted. I do remember the circumstances surrounding the day very well. It was what I would have called a bad day. Tears were frequent and the despair of missing Daniel was unbearable. I remember thinking that the one good thing was, it is a beautiful day. The temperature was mild for a summer day and the humidity was nearly nothing at all. I decided to go outside and sit on my deck in the backyard. I was sure the fresh air and the great weather would do me good. Even though I was outside I was reminded of Daniel everywhere I looked. The tree brought back memories of watching him climb to the very top without any fear and wanting him to hurry up and climb down. The backyard brought back so many sweet memories of him playing football, soccer and anything else that may have involved running. I had my feet propped up on the railing of the deck. All my thoughts were centered on Daniel and the grief I was feeling as I sat there. I soon noticed a beautiful yellow butterfly sitting very close to my foot that was still propped up on the deck railing. I quickly became very interested in this butterfly because I was surprised at how long it just sat there and how totally unafraid it seemed to be. I moved my foot and was even more surprised that I had not startled it and it still remained on the railing. Needless to say the awe of this butterfly took my mind off of Daniel because I was enjoying this little piece of nature very much. The little butterfly stayed for a long time and I felt a peace and a calmness that I needed greatly that day. I am discovering that the smallest moments of joy or happiness must be cherished and not taken for granted. I was grateful for the little yellow butterfly that had decided to land in my backyard when I was out there. The little butterfly helped me not to feel so sad because it had diverted my attention away from thinking about Daniel.

It was over a month when a yellow butterfly made another appearance. It was the morning we were leaving for Hawaii. Our family had boarded the plane and we had taxied out onto the runway. Jenny was sitting by a window, I was in the middle seat and Matt was in the aisle seat. Karl, Amy and Michael were in the seats across the aisle from us. Jenny turned to me with big tears in her eyes and said, "I wish Daniel were going with us on this family vacation. He is supposed to be going with us." I told Jenny if there was any way that Daniel could be with us I was sure he would be here even if it wasn't his physical body going with us now. Our plane had come to a stop on the tarmac as we waited for our turn to take off. Suddenly I heard Jenny say, "Mom, look! It's a yellow butterfly!" A yellow butterfly had landed on the outside of her window's edge. I couldn't believe it. Over a month ago I had told the family of my experience with the butterfly on the deck. I now questioned if my earlier experience with the butterfly was more than just an encounter with nature. One would never expect to find a butterfly on a runway and yet this one was not only on an airport runway but it had landed on the plane window. A butterfly on a runway seemed like a rather amazing thing but add the fact that it landed on Jenny's window. Of all the numerous windows on our airplane it chose Jenny's window. I needed comfort when I sat on the deck and a butterfly appeared. Jenny wanted comfort because she was so sad at the thought that Daniel wasn't with us on our family vacation that had been planned long before Daniel died. I told Jenny that maybe Daniel sent us a butterfly to let us know he is here for us and he isn't very far away.

It was in the spring of 2004 that the third appearance of a yellow butterfly appeared to Karl. At the time Karl was going through a stage of anger towards Daniel. He decided one afternoon to go to the marina and work on the sailboat. Being around boats and on the water has always been a great stress reducer for Karl. I knew he had been having a rough time in the last few days so I was glad he wanted to go to the marina. After several hours he called to tell me that he wasn't angry anymore at Daniel. I thought great; I knew being around his boat would help. When I made the comment to him with the reference of being on the boat being the best therapy for him he said it was more than that. He then began to tell me another incredible story that dealt with a yellow butterfly. He said he had spent the majority of his time down below the deck fixing the bilge pump. As usual he had left the cabin door open for light and fresh air. Even as he is working on the pump he is thinking of Daniel and the anger he feels towards him. He doesn't understand the anger because we have both talked about it on many occasions. We both easily get mad at Daniel for what he has done but we never stay mad long. We don't stay mad because we know Daniel never intended to hurt us and he too was in a lot of pain and misery for him to do what he did. Karl said while he was working he felt as if he were talking to Daniel and trying to work his way through the anger. He had to pull back from the small space where the bilge pump was located to get a tool and the new part. As he reached for the tool on the table he was shocked to see a beautiful yellow butterfly sitting directly on top of his navigation table. He too is very familiar with the past encounters with a yellow butterfly. He immediately thinks of Daniel and thinks Daniel doesn't want me to be mad at him anymore. Then he realizes there is a yellow butterfly inside the cabin of his sailboat. He can't believe it! Never has he seen a butterfly near a marina, and boats. And yet here sits a gorgeous yellow butterfly sitting inside his boat. Once again you are reminded of all the many boats that are docked at this marina and a yellow butterfly chooses Karl's boat to come inside and land on the table where Karl would definitely see it. Is this a mere coincidence?

This afternoon Karl and I were sitting on the front porch and the little MR2 was parked directly in front of us. Karl has driven the car since it was repaired and he has very tender feelings towards that car. He feels a connection with that car. He says the car is his linking object to Daniel. Joe is in need of a car because the only transportation he has is his bike at the university. Karl has been thinking of giving the car to Joe. As we were sitting on the porch Karl is telling me that he thinks it is going to be hard to hand over the car to Joe. It's not that he doesn't want Joe to have it but he feels it will be hard to not have the car around and be able to drive it whenever he wants. Karl feels a real closeness to Daniel whenever he drives the car. That's understandable because Daniel cared so much about his car. As we are sitting on the porch a beautiful yellow butterfly flies to the back of Daniel's car and lands on the back of the trunk. We both look at each other and smile. Karl says, "I guess that's it. Daniel is telling me it's ok to let Joe have the car because he needs a car."

We as a family now notice yellow butterflies. Every time I see a yellow butterfly I do not automatically think that it is Daniel sending me some sort of message. The yellow butterflies came when they were needed in our lives. Now I have a love for the butterflies because of the symbol they represent. I have no way of knowing if Daniel sent those yellow butterflies on those four different occasions, I would like to think he did. I don't even think it matters now because the purpose was met at the time of the greatest need. We now love to mention to each other when we see yellow butterflies. It is a sweet reminder that we each think of Daniel when we see a yellow butterfly and we still miss him terribly.

There have been three other events involving electricity that I have failed to write about. All three happened very shortly after his death. The first was at Daniel's funeral. As Joe was about half way through giving the eulogy he began to break down and suddenly the power went completely out in the whole church for about a minute and a half. I sat there and prayed for God to give him strength to carry on. I have been attending church in this building for almost 10 years and have never had this happen before. It was not raining or storming outside and there is no apparent reason for the power to have gone out. Joe regained composure and continued without the microphone and the only source of light was from the chapel windows. As he continued the power eventually came back on as mysteriously as it went out. After the funeral service many commented that they had never seen the power go out in that building during a meeting.

The second time I was not at home, Karl was working in the home office and Jenny was upstairs getting dressed. Jenny thought about wearing one of Daniel's belts so she went to Daniels room to see if she could find it. She found the belt and as she was putting it through her belt loops she realized that if Daniel were alive he would have never allowed her wear it. She broke down in tears as she was wishing that he were here to stop her. As she was looking around the room at all of Daniel's things she began to miss him terribly and began to sob and tell him out loud how much she truly missed him. It was at that moment that the electricity in the house went out. Jenny was left in the dark except for the light that was coming in from a small window. As Karl came out of the home office to find out why the electricity went out he ran into Jenny who had left Daniel's room because she felt his presence and she got scared. When I got home Karl was eager to tell me that he had felt Daniel's presence in the house that afternoon.

The third time involved his best friend at one of Daniel's favorite restaurants. A group of Daniels friends had just been seated. The conversation quickly turned to Daniel because all knew this was Daniel's favorite restaurant. Daniel's best friend told me that as fond memories were being shared the tears began to fall. The electricity went out and the emergency exit lights all come on. The waitress came and said that this had never happened before and they would have to leave. As the friends began to exit, the restaurant's lights came back on. They were then invited to return to their table. Someone commented that Daniel must have done it so they wouldn't be sitting around and crying over him. His friend was eager to tell us that an incident had happened which was like the one that had happened at the funeral with the electricity.

I don't know why these things happen but for whatever reason they are just more signs that there is more to life than we understand.

September 9, 2004
"Birthdays are still hard"

Today marks the second birthday that I have now spent without celebrating it with Daniel. As a mother your children's birthdays are very special days. It is the one day that truly connects you with a physical bond to your child. Daniel is my son because I gave birth to him on this date. The birthday of a deceased child brings it so clearly in the fore front of your mind of how wrong this all is. Parents are not meant to bury their children. Children are meant to have many more birthdays after their own parents have left this life. I am a daughter who lost her father at seventeen years of age. Every year on January eleventh I think of my dad's birthday and try to remember how old he would have been if he were still alive. I am now up to eighty three years old. I know there will reach a year when I feel surely he would have already passed on. I would like to think that if his health had been better he would still be alive today to see and love his precious and wonderful grandchildren and great grandchildren. As an adult who has lost a parent you know that your parents will die someday. There will come a day when a special occasion will have to be celebrated without them such as their birthdays. As a parent you never think about or can even imagine having your child's birthday without him or her here to celebrate it with them. Birthdays are hard and I think they will only get harder as the years continue to roll on by. In my mind each year I will think about how old he would have been and what he would have probably been doing if he were still alive. Parents are there to celebrate their children's successes of graduating from college, getting married, having children, watching their careers flourish and all the other numerous milestones that occur. If Daniel is not here to leave his mark in this world who will remember him when his parents are gone? My greatest fear is Daniel will be forgotten after Karl and I are no longer here to make sure he isn't forgotten.

December 29, 2004
"easier than last year"

The second holiday season was better than the first. I still was not ready to be home for the holidays. The holidays were not easy but they were easier than last year. There is something to be said about getting through that first year. I am no expert by any means and as of yet I have no time under my belt but I do know that the first year was terrible for me.

It was in the early fall that Laurie mentioned that she would like to take her children to Disney World. As we began to list all the different expenses we realized that it was very possible that we could go for Christmas if we all pooled our money together. The moms had already decided that the children had enough toys and didn't need anymore. The money that would have been spent on gifts for everyone could be used for Disney World. So that is what we did. The distraction of being away from home is what I needed once again to help me focus on Daniel not being here at Christmas time. I loved being with the children and grandchildren. I have got to realize that when you have a big gaping hole in your heart a little band-aid isn't going to fix it. It doesn't matter where you go or how far you go it is still Christmas time and Daniel isn't here with us. The thing that I did like was the fact that I wasn't at home where the memories are so vivid.

January 20, 2005
"waiting for the other shoe to drop"

There is one thing that you certainly realize as a mother of a son who has killed himself. You live with this dreaded fear of waiting for the other shoe to drop. Before Daniel's death I had fears and concerns for my children but it is nothing compared to what goes on in my head now. I was on my way home earlier this morning from running errands when I came upon an accident. Now before Daniel's death I would have felt concern and sympathy for the victims in the accident and certainly would hope all would be well with them. This morning I see the blue flashing lights and an ambulance up ahead of me. My thoughts now go immediately to my family. I become extremely interested in seeing the make and model of the car or cars involved in the accident. I quickly realize that it is not one of our family cars then I race through my memory bank to remember my children's friend's cars. It's not a panic feeling but I know it's a feeling of over concern. It's as if before Daniel's death I knew accidents could happen but now I really know that horrible things can happen to my family. Bad things can happen to me and if it happened once then it is possible that things can happen again.

I would be lying if I said that I never think about my other children killing themselves. You live with that all the time. I am so honest when I tell you I never once thought of Daniel being suicidal but with great sadness I know he was, after the fact. So now I know it can happen and I fear what would keep the other children from acting out their own thoughts. Daniel is our proof that it can happen in this family. There is a part of me that wants to think there is no way that any one of them could subject their family to such a horrible tragedy ever again. These children have seen for themselves the horrible loss we have felt as parents and siblings. They each know first hand what this loss has done to our family but I also know suicide is not about rational thinking or thinking in the future about the pain that suicide brings to the remaining loved ones. I have always believed that Daniel would have never killed himself if he had known the enormous pain he would be causing his family.

I have a great deal of fear when the children (I speak of the teenagers who are living at home) get mad and the emotions begin to run high as you would expect when tempers flare. I have fear when teenagers get mad, storm off and shut their bedroom doors. This is a horrible side effect that parents must endure who have lost a child to suicide. I wish there were a time line that would say expect this reaction for this amount of time. I guess this is like grief. Everyone is different and there are no rules or absolutes as to how grief will affect a person. My therapist once told me that when I am in that state of fear I am going from a tiny little mole hill to MT Everest. It's as if the event would be described by the majority of the world as a fire cracker and I've reacted as if the event is an atomic bomb. So when a teenager storms out of a heated conversation the fear kicks in. It is such irrational thinking. I very easily understand that teenagers and parents have heated moments. I am the mother of eight children and Daniel was number five. Four other teenage children have successfully passed through the doors to adulthood. I have for sure seen my share of disputes with teenagers. I never had such fear with any of them. In fact when they went storming out of a room it was probably a feeling of relief. I figured we both needed to just back away from the moment and cool off. Now they storm off and I go from being angry to being fearful. Especially if I hear their bedroom doors shut. My mind starts racing. What are they doing behind the doors, what are they thinking. I have lots and lots of questions concerning Daniel's suicide. I know he was in a state of rage and anger when he killed himself. So naturally I think about suicide when my other children storm off and lock themselves in their bedrooms. Before Daniel's death this act of getting mad and going into their bedroom and locking their door would have been described by me as a typical reaction of a teenager. Now that is no longer true. I go from a reaction of a firecracker to the atomic bomb. I do not do anything that is physical that would be a true indicator of what is going on in my head. It is just that my mind is racing with hundreds of thoughts of doom until I go to them and see for myself that they are fine. Usually they are still angry but definitely not in danger to themselves. There was one family rule that had to be made soon after Daniel's death. The children who still live at home have been very good at helping us keep this new rule. We have asked the children if they lock their doors to change clothes to please remember to unlock the doors. Locked bedroom doors are a very scary thing to experience in this house. Remember it was behind a locked bedroom door that we found Daniel. I remember one time when I went to Jenny's room to wake her in the morning for school and her door was locked. I knocked and there was no answer. I called out and believe me she didn't answer fast enough. My heart began to race and I knew I was at the throws of a panic attack. I could tell by the look on her face when she finally awoke and opened her door that she knew I was afraid. I knew she saw fear on my face because she grabbed me, took me in her arms and said, "Mom, its ok. I am ok."

Chapter 13
year 2 - Month 30

"Thinking of him"

February 17, 2005
"Daniel is nearby"

It is just so endless. It never takes a break for very long. Grief, my constant companion who has been with me for one year, fifty weeks and two days. I really don't count weeks and days to that degree but perhaps if I were ever quizzed then I would even surprise myself that I could readily give someone how long it had been since Daniel died. I only know in two weeks it will be the second anniversary of Daniel's death. Perhaps this is the reason for so many tears and endless thoughts of him today. I answered the phone this morning to have a married daughter ask with a chuckle in her voice and yet a sincere desire to know if we felt that Daniel was near by. I knew exactly what she meant. It's a definite feeling that you cannot describe. She said she had been thinking about Daniel all the time lately and this is not something that occurs for her on a daily basis. She is constantly thinking about him. It's during these times you can question the other family members and we all have the same feedback. Daniel is being constantly thought about day after day by us all and it will last for a fair amount of time. The feelings are very real and yet they can't be adequately described. I honestly feel as though he is nearby and is with us. I wish I could say I see him or even hear him but I don't. We just know he is around us. One may easily rationalize that the feelings of him being so near would have to be because we are thinking about him all the time and he is in the forethoughts of all our minds. But it is so much more than that because we are also very aware of the void when he isn't close by. Perhaps he feels our anxiousness of the upcoming anniversary of his death. He knows we are saddened deeply of the thoughts that we miss him so much and it has been two years since we saw that cute smile on such a good looking young boy.

This second anniversary is hard for me for a specific reason. I have had the experience as a mother to send two nineteen year old sons on missions for our church. They fulfill a mission for two years and return home. I did not see either son for two years while they were away. Each homecoming was a joyous and wonderful experience. I am now approaching the two year mark of not seeing Daniel. I want so desperately to be planning a well celebrated homecoming for a returned missionary. It's been two years and he left us at nineteen years old. It's now time for celebrating the glorious homecoming. I have close friends who have sons who are now returning from their missions. I am happy for them because I know what it feels like to have a son return from a mission. But I want so much for this third son to be on his way home too. I find great comfort in knowing he will have an even greater homecoming than I could ever dream possible when I one day go home to him.

March 1, 2005
"looking for gifts"

One thing I have learned for sure is to always look for the gifts and to be ever so grateful when they come your way. Since the death of Daniel I would have to say that my sweetest gifts would have to be when I was blessed to dream about Daniel. Every night when I say my prayers I ask Heavenly Father if I should dream about Daniel to please let me remember dreaming about him. This morning I remember in complete detail my dream about Daniel. It was wonderful, glorious and oh so sweet. I did not recognize where I was standing but I was inside a building. Daniel came around a corner and went rushing by me. I was so thrilled to see him. I called out his name and he kept going. It was easy to tell he was in a very big hurry to get somewhere. I called out to him again and he stopped. I have never seen him look so happy! He had his famous grin and seemed just as excited to see me too. He was wearing a pair of perfectly tailored khaki pants, and a beautifully ironed long-sleeved white shirt with a button down collar. His sleeves were rolled part way up his forearms. He was carrying a small black planner that was unzipped. His appearance gave me the immediate impression that he was working and was extremely busy! Whenever I have dreamt about him in the past as soon I have touched him I immediately wake up. In my dream this morning I start walking towards him and I have a little fear because I know I can't touch him. It's as if I know if I touch him then I will no longer be in his presence. As I start going towards him he looks directly in my eyes and says to me, "Mom, you can't touch me." I answer back, "I know but I have to." As I am reaching for him he is saying, "Mom, don't touch me." Daniel was about 6'1" or 6'2" tall so when I would hug him my head would always be pressed against his chest. In my dream I grab hold of him and my head is pressing into his chest. It is the most wonderful and special feeling. I feel his hands coming up and rubbing the back of my head as he presses me into his chest harder. I immediately woke up. My eyes were full of tears just as they were when I was dreaming of him holding me. I was so happy because it felt as though I just had a visit with him even though it was way too short. But a visit with Daniel at this point would never be long enough. I was grateful that I had remembered the dream in such detail. I loved the way he looked. I have never seen Daniel look so happy and he looked older. I remember his strong looking arms as they appeared from the rolled up shirt sleeves. His face looked radiant and his face looked like that of an older person not a young nineteen year old teenager. I will forever remember looking into his face and seeing how happy he was and knowing with such surety that he is about some very serious business.

I also had tears this morning because seeing him even in a dream makes it so real how much I miss him and want to be physically near him again. I also gave thanks for another very special reason this morning. I got to see Daniel on March 1st. I have had regrets and sadness that I never saw or spoke to Daniel on March 1st the day before he died. I am so glad that even if it was a dream I got to see and talk to Daniel on March 1st. Last year I relived the last couple days of Daniel's life in my mind as March 2nd approached. Last year I knew that on March 1, 2003 I had not seen Daniel on that day. Now today instead of being so sad that I did not see him the day before he died I have a beautiful dream to reflect upon. Yes, it may have only been in a dream but it was definitely a beautiful dream in which I saw and spoke to Daniel on a new March 1st. For that I will always be grateful for today's wonderful gift.

March 3, 2005
"feeding alligators"

The anniversary went better than I thought it would go. Once again it is the anticipation that is worse. The leading up to that date is far worse than actually living through the day. This seems to be the norm of how it has been with previous anniversary dates that deal with Daniel's death. Karl was not home and he had so many concerns about not being here with me. He was very hesitant about not being with me on March 2nd. Joe who is a senior at the University of FL will be graduating in a couple of months. He had wanted to canoe and camp in the Everglades National Park before he graduated and left Florida. Karl was concerned and would prefer that Joe not go alone. In Joe's email to his dad he seems happy that his dad has offered to go with him but with what felt like hesitation told his dad the dates. Joe's spring break would be the first week of March and if his dad went they would be gone March 2nd. Karl and I discussed it and easily agreed that he needed to go. What was he going to do? Go with me to the cemetery put flowers on the marker and stand there and cry as we had done last year. I told him I would be ok. It was far more important to me that he go with our living son and make beautiful memories together than stay home and cry over Daniel. I knew that would be what Daniel would have done. As much as that kid loved high adventure and anything outdoors I knew he would have never given up an opportunity to canoe in the Everglades. Once Karl was at ease about leaving me it became fun to watch him and see his excitement. He packed days before he left and bought so many things that would make the trip fun including a very nice hand held GPS. It became very apparent that this was exactly what he needed to be doing. Karl did suggest to Joe one small change in plans. Karl was afraid that one day in the Everglades would look like the next and the next and the next! So he suggested that they camp for five days and spend two days on the golf courses. Joe is becoming quite the golfer so there was little need to do anything but mention it to Joe and he was all for the couple days of golf.

Karl had asked what I thought I would do on the 2nd and I wasn't sure. Karl said in honor of Daniel he was going to feed an alligator on March 2nd and he would laugh while he was doing it because he was positive that Daniel would be laughing right along with him. I too laughed when he said it because there sure is a lot of truth in that statement and there is a great story about Daniel and alligators. When Daniel was 10 years old we lived in Goose Creek, SC. We lived in Navy officer housing and there was a nice big golf course near our house. Daniel and Michael would go out on the golf course to look for golf balls. They had learned from children in the neighborhood to take the golf balls to the club house and sell them to the golfers for 25 cents a piece. On this golf course there were a couple of lakes and they found the most golf balls near these lakes. Why, because the golfers knew the lakes had alligators and no golfer wanted to go near the lake for a golf ball? One day while riding home from church Karl and I are listening to Daniel tell a story that involves an alligator. At first we thought he was telling about something he has seen on TV. We realize later in the story that this is an actual event involving Daniel. Karl tells Daniel as soon as we get home he is to change his clothes and take him to the place he is talking about. I decide to go along too. We take the paved road around the edge of the golf course and at a certain point Daniel tells us to stop the car and we have to walk down this dirt path. As Karl and I are walking we are looking at each other in total disbelief. We are looking at this lake in front of us and we can actually see alligators sunning themselves on the bank on the other side. The alligators see us and two of them slide into the water and start swimming towards the side of the lake we are on. Karl said "do you believe this? There is no fence or wall of any kind between us and the alligators." The story only gets better when Daniel informs us that the alligator swimming towards us is the mama. He says there is a real cute baby somewhere because one day he had to grab his luncheon meat off the ground really fast to keep the mama from getting it so he could feed the baby. Well, at this point I am sure I have turned just as white as Karl because all the color has left Karl's face and both our mouths have dropped to what felt like the ground. We both at the exact same time told Daniel to get in the car and to hurry up. He tells us that he and Michael have learned from their new friends to never run in a straight line because alligators are very fast. That you must run fast but run in a zigzag pattern because alligators can't turn fast. When we finally arrive safely in our car, Karl tells Daniel that his new playground has been permanently closed. He is never to come here again nor look for golf balls to sell. And to think we just thought they were walking on the golf course that was only a street over from our house. Thank goodness Daniel's new playground had been discovered by us in a short amount of time after we moved there. So in honor of Daniel, Karl will feed the alligators for Daniel one more time. But, as it turned out, they never saw an alligator or even a snake.

On the morning of March 2nd I went to the florist and bought white roses for the marker. I love white roses and the feeling of peace I get when I look at them. Missy had called and had planned to come over in the afternoon but that didn't work out. Jenny, Laurie, two of the grandchildren and I went out to lunch. It was a very good thing to be with them and I was thrilled to have my children near me and I wasn't by myself. I love my family so much! Late in the afternoon when Amy got home she asked if we could go out to get something for dinner. It was a good excuse not to cook. I checked in with all the children to see how they were doing and how they had spent the day. Amy said her day was sad but she was also glad that she had spent so much of the day thinking about Daniel. I am so glad that even today two years later we still talk about Daniel all the time and we are all very open about our feelings towards Daniel's death. I really believe that talking and crying is all part of the long journey called healing.

April 2, 2005
"thoughts of Daniel"

I had joy today and it was a great feeling. I had joy in realizing that there has been tremendous growth in my journey of grief. What I had hoped and prayed for two years ago is coming to pass. I had a soul purpose in beginning this journal on Daniel's death. I wanted to reach a time and a place that I literally saw improvement in my grieving process. My journal who now feels like an old friend has helped to bring me to this place I am now in. I can read the entries that were written long ago and I immediately feel the pain that was expressed on those journal pages. But it is with a feeling of joy that I realize that I am no longer in those horrible, wretched pains of grief that had totally consumed me and made me feel as though I were a prisoner in my own body. I wanted desperately to be released from such a frightening grip but felt so powerless over such overwhelming feelings. Today I am able to function in a far better mode and capacity than ever before since the journey began in March 2003. I don't know when the magical day arrived but I now know that I am going to survive. For over two years I have been telling myself that I was going to survive this even though I had no idea how it was going to be possible. Perhaps it was mind over matter and the power of positive suggestion. I suppose I believed if I told myself enough times then it was bound to happen.

I recently heard a very interesting comment made by a famous person. Ed McMahon was talking about his dear friend Johnny Carson who had recently passed away. In his comments he said he and Johnny Carson shared the experience of losing a child. Johnny Carson had lost his son several years before Ed McMahon's son had died. I had gotten the impression that it has also been some time since his son had died. Johnny told Ed that even though his son was dead he would still think about him everyday. Not a day would go by that he wouldn't think of his loss. Ed McMahon commented on how true it was that a day never passes that he doesn't think about the death of his son.

It has only been two years and I know for myself that I have thought of Daniel everyday and expect that I will as long as I live. I am so grateful that now I can think of Daniel with happy memories and of happier days. Now my thoughts of Daniel are not always laced with sadness and remorse. Oh sure, I still miss him tremendously and my heart still hurts because I don't physically have him in my life. There is some truth in the statement that time heals all wounds. I know I am not completely healed but I do know I am healing and it is a nice feeling to be in a healing stage and not in a place of utter pain and torment where I was two years ago.

September 9, 2005
"birthdays are still hard"

I doubt that there was even one minute that I didn't think about Daniel yesterday. I awoke this morning in the very early hours of dawn and he came to my mind immediately. Today is his birthday and birthdays are hard. All day yesterday and many days prior I thought about him being twenty-two years old today. I reflect on the older children who have already celebrated their 22nd birthday. Twenty-two years old and beyond are good years and especially for parents. They have successfully made it through the sometimes difficult teenage years. Young adults are beginning to find themselves and settling down to the routines of life whether it be a career or continuing on with their education. One of the great things that I have discovered as a mother of older children is how much fun they are to be around. The role of parent to child changes a great deal. You are no longer there to offer physical parenting. Adult children are very enjoyable to be around. These same children who only a few years earlier in their teenage years thought they knew everything and you knew nothing have now changed their minds. They realize parents aren't so dumb after all and they are not as smart as they were so sure they were. These adult children actually enjoy our company. How nice it is to be sitting in a room and they come to sit with me just to be social and are generally interested in what is going on in my life. They haven't come to ask for money or ask permission to go somewhere or do something. That teenage phase in their life is now over and the self centeredness and the world revolves around me stage is over. Daniel was never a difficult teenager to parent. We had the typical parent and teenager confrontations but he was easy to talk to and he was a good listener. Of course now with 20/20 hindsight I wish he were a better talker. I wish he were here today to celebrate his 22nd birthday and I want him here to celebrate many more birthdays. I want to sit with a young twenty two year old son and have him tell me how he is doing and what is new in his life. I want to hear his views about what is going on in the world today. I want to talk about current events with this young adult who is suppose to be here and should outlive his mother. Yes, birthdays are hard and it is another painful reminder that he is no longer here.

I can remember when Daniel was a little boy he came to me with excitement in his voice. He had come to the great realization that he was going to have a birthday on 9-9-09. He was going to be twenty-six years old on September 9,

2009. He thought that was going to be the neatest thing in the world to have a birthday on 9-9-09. He even asked me if I would give him a really big birthday party that year. I can remember telling him that by the time we got to 2009 he would probably be married and have a family of his own. I told him that I felt sure his wife would give him a big birthday party but I would ask if I could help her. Daniel seemed quite pleased and content with my answer. I don't know where I am going to be on 9-9-09 but I do feel very strongly that wherever it may be I am going to be celebrating. I am going to have that party for Daniel.

Chapter 14
Month 32 - year 3

"The final Chapter"

October 13, 2005
"what have I done"

I write this entry today about a very significant event that occurred over seven months ago. In fact it was on March 2nd, the second anniversary of his death. I have known for a long time that this had to be written. I know if this journal had actual chapters this would be the final chapter. I have also known that this chapter had to be written if I were ever to move on and find closure in my life. I am not sure why there is so much trepidation in writing this other than the fact it means the end.

As I met with my therapist right before the March 2nd anniversary approached I expressed to her that I had a very intense feeling that I wanted to speak with Daniel's girlfriend. I wanted closure and I knew I had to talk to her. From day one I have felt that she was my ace in the hole. If I could talk to her then I could finally get answers as to why. It was the day after Daniel's death when I asked Daniel's dearest friend if he knew how she was doing. I sent word to her that if she wanted to come by she was welcome to come to our home. She came the next day. I heard she had arrived and I found her in my dining room. I remember going to her and giving her a hug. I pulled her away from me so I could look directly in her eyes. I wanted her to see my eyes, look into my soul if she could.

As I looked into her eyes I told her this was not her fault and that she must never blame herself for this. That was the last time I had seen her or spoken to her.

Even though two years has now passed I still had those same feelings. I wanted her to know I had no hard feelings toward her. It became very important to me to let her know that I truly did want her to be happy. In the past two years I have heard little things about how she was doing but nothing directly from her. My therapist asked if I were to meet with her what would I say. My first response was to ask if Daniel had ever said anything about wanting to die. Had he ever said anything that would make her think he was depressed or suicidal? I told my therapist that I was afraid that one day I would make the attempt to get in touch with her and I would not be able to find her. She told me in today's world with so much technology it would be difficult to totally lose contact with her. It may be in years to come because of distance that I may not be able to speak with her face to face and it may need to be thru letters or the internet. She suggested that I practice what I would say to her by writing it in a letter. Even if I had zero intentions of mailing it I could still write down my thoughts.

As I drove home from my appointment my mind was flooded with thoughts of why am I waiting? What purpose was I serving by waiting other than I had a lot of fear on my part? I decided I would write the letter and see what happens. I drove to the Hallmark store to look for a card. I quickly decided on a card that was blank on the inside. Then it became ridiculous how I agonized over what type of front to choose from. I was concerned that the front might send the wrong message. How that was going to happen I have no idea. I finally decided on a card that had a beautiful yellow rose on the front and had a sheer ribbon tied on the side of the card. As soon as I got home I went to the computer and began my rough draft of the letter. I liked the wording so I transposed it to the card. A few weeks ago my therapist had told me about a way to find a person's address by using reverse look up on the computer. Still attached to the inside of my kitchen cabinet was an old list of phone numbers. What now seems like a very long time ago Daniel had written her phone number on the bottom of the sheet in case we needed to get in touch with him while he was at her house. He never did get a cell phone even though he had talked about it. Even though I had been to her house once to pick Daniel up when his car was broke I could no longer remember the name of the street she lived on. Plus it was midnight when I picked him up and I wasn't sure I could find the house again even by driving around. This web site works very well. As soon as I put her phone number in her address came up and I recognized it immediately as the name of the street she lived on. Not only did I write the card but I addressed it. I had chosen to do this task at my dining room table. As I sealed the envelope I looked out the dining room front window and saw the mail carrier at our mailbox. I quickly grabbed the stamp sitting on the table and hurried out the door to hand the card to our mail carrier. As I walked back into my house I certainly questioned what on earth had I just done. I thought for about ten seconds of tracking him down and asking for my card back but I decided against it. My legs felt really heavy as I walked up the steps and into my front door. It felt like a long walk back from the mailbox. What have I done was all I could think about. Karl was in FL camping with Joe with no cell phone service so I couldn't even tell him what had just taken place.

In this card to her I expressed my desire to get in touch with her. I told her it had been too long since we last talked and it was way overdue. I had questions and I felt she may have questions too. I told her that if she prefer her mother meet with us also that would be fine with me. I also let her know if she chose not to get in touch with me that I would understand that also. In closing I gave her several ways to get in touch with me including my cell phone number. Once again I let her know by writing in the card that I didn't blame her for Daniel's death and this meeting would not be about any such matter.

Laurie had asked that we go out to lunch on March 2nd since she knew her dad was out of town on Daniel's second anniversary of his death. I greatly appreciated the invitation because I wasn't looking forward to being by myself on that particular day. Jenny and two of Laurie's youngest children went with us. It was a great distraction and I love any occasion when I am with my family. On the day before I had included Daniel's girlfriend's phone number in my cell phone. I wanted it to show up on caller ID if she were to call. I wanted to know if it was her before I answered and not be taken by total surprise if she ever decided to call me. When I got in my car to go home from my lunch date I checked my cell phone. I saw I had a missed call and it was from her. I was so surprised! It had been less than twenty-four hours since I had mailed the card and I was already hearing from her. There was no message and I decided not to return the call until I got home. As I was driving home my phone rang again and it was her home phone number on the caller ID. I answered it and it was her mother. She was calling for her daughter and yes they would like to see me. So soon in fact that it was agreed upon that very afternoon. I drove home and got a small gift that I wanted her to have. It is a picture of Daniel that is my favorite. The summer before he died we took a family vacation to Niagara Falls. As Daniel stood at the railing overlooking the falls Karl took a great picture. There is no railing to be seen in the picture but lots of mist and spray is the back ground of the picture. As I look at this picture today it has taken on a totally different meaning than it did when he was alive. It now looks as though he is looking down from heaven through the clouds to check on us. I love this picture of him very much and have had several copies made. I have never doubted how much Daniel loved this girl. I have always known there was an enormous amount of love towards her so I figured he too would look down on her to check on her. I had a small frame that I put the picture in and I got directions to her house from Map quest. I was very nervous and anxious because I knew it was time. I personally needed this meeting with her in order for me to move on in my journey.

It was obvious that we were both very nervous with the idle chit chat that was taking place in the beginning. Her mother was sitting with us in their family room and I was fine with the arrangement. After twenty or so minutes I realized the small talk was nice but this was far from the real reason I was there. I moved the conversation to the real reason I was there. I came right out and asked her if Daniel had ever said he wished he were dead, or talked about dying? Had she ever noticed any signs of depression with Daniel? Her immediate answer was no, never had any of those thoughts or feelings ever transpired between the two of them. She also said that if she were to list all her friends that Daniel would be the very last on her list to have thought of suicide much less to have followed through with it.

At this time I wish not to disclose the entire conversation that transpired between the two of us. Very soon into the meeting I realized I would never know the exact words that were spoken between her and Daniel that Sunday morning. Both mother and daughter seemed to be very guarded in their conversation in talking about what transpired Sunday morning. It was the way they almost seemed to be catching themselves before they said too much. But I knew something had been said to Daniel that shook his soul. I will never know the exact words but I do know words were spoken that shattered him. My main purpose for going was to see if I could find out what had happened that Sunday morning between the two of them. I found my answer and yet I have no real details and that isn't important to me any longer. The cause will never change the outcome. I can not bring Daniel back. It is almost as if I have known the answer from the beginning. Daniel loved this girl very much, so much so that he literally couldn't imagine life without her. I will never blame her for Daniel's death. I do know something happened between them on the Sunday morning he died that caused him to go to a place that he had never been before. A place that had so much pain for him that he would have rather died than feel another moment of pain that he was currently experiencing.

I turned the conversation in a direction that I wanted to go. I found out how often she visits the cemetery and was amazed that we haven't run into each other. I can bet there were days we passed each other either going or coming. I asked if she ever dreamed about Daniel and she said yes. I loved it when she said they were car dreams. That was one reason Daniel was so taken with her. She loved cars too and knew lots about sports cars. She told me there were times she felt him near by. I told her I didn't know how it all works but I knew Daniel cared so much about her and if ever there was a way for him to come back and check on her I was sure he would. I then gave her the picture and told her the story of why it was important to me. Perhaps she too will look at this picture and feel as though he is looking down from heaven to see her too.

Before I left I asked that she do me a favor. I asked her to be happy. I wanted her to have the life that Daniel never had. I wanted her to continue with her education, get married, have children and live the best possible life. She would make me happy if I knew she did something with her life and was happy. We hugged each other as I departed to go back home.

I was very happy that I went to see her. She is not on my list to send a Christmas card nor will I be inviting her over for Sunday dinner but I definitely do not have any ill feelings toward her. If she were to appear on my doorstep today I would invite her into my home as a welcomed guest. She is a mere child and a tragic event has occurred in her life. For this I am very sorry. Just as I feel for my children I also feel very sad for her that she has had to experience this tragedy in her young life. I have the greatest sadness for Daniel. Girls break up with boys all the time and hurting words are spoken between couples but thank God people don't kill themselves every time there is a break up in a relationship. I wish Daniel could have known that it would have been all right in a very short amount of time. It may have been extremely painful at that moment but if he had just waited a little longer he would have seen it was all going to be ok and most importantly he was going to be ok and life goes on.

Life certainly does go on even though our cherished children may have gone on before us. It has now become a life that I would never wish on my worst enemy. It is a life that has now experienced the most unbelievable amount of pain. Only God could create a body that could endure so much pain and heartache and still survive. There has not been one day that I have not thought of Daniel and the tremendous loss I feel for him. I know the giant hole in my heart will always be there until I am back in his presence. My journey is nowhere complete. I am still *searching for my new normal.* I have accepted the fact that my life will never be as it was before March 2, 2003. I still cry for Daniel but I don't cry everyday. I can now talk about Daniel without crying and I can look at his pictures and look directly at his eyes and not cry.

I still have the question of why and I have to come to realize that it is ok to ask why. As I stated in the beginning I would not accept his answer even if he stood before me and told me why. It is for this reason that I no longer dwell on the "why" every waking minute of the day as I have done in the past. My heart is now filled with three questions. I want to know if he regrets it and is he sorry for the heartache and pain he has caused his family. In my heart I already know the answers to the first two questions because I know my child so very well. The third question I would ask is of the utmost importance to me. The question concerns his happiness. I once read a quote by Marjorie Hinckley that I love very much. She said, "I am only as happy as my saddest child." I want to know that Daniel is happy and even if he were given the choice he would not come back because of such happiness he is feeling now.

My heart tells me he is in far better place even though I want to argue with anyone that tells me that. I want him here with me because that is where I feel he belongs. There are some things that have come to me from this tragedy. I definitely know God lives and He knows me and knows of this great loss I am feeling. He is with me in every step that I take. He has never left my side. I also know that Daniel still lives. His body died on March 2, 2003 but his spirit is very much alive. Daniel is about living. Daniel is so much more than that one afternoon on March 2nd. Daniel lived! Now I too must live. Pain is a given under the circumstances of losing a child but misery is an option. I choose to live a decent life for myself and my family. I owe this to myself, my family and I owe it to Daniel as well. It has been a long and very difficult road that I have traveled in the last two and a half years. I am grateful for the place that I am currently in and I look forward to the place I'll be in another two, or five, or ten or twenty years from now. I am grateful that I sat down and began this journal seven days after Daniel died. I can read that first entry today and realize how much I have forgotten about the details of the day he died. I can read that entry now and immediately be transported to that very afternoon. The pain is just as fresh as if it all just happened. When I revisit those early days and weeks by reading my journal I feel the pain because I remember what I was feeling when I wrote it. Thank God that today my life is not gripped with that awful, debilitating pain. There is something that seems to take place around two years. I was told by professionals as well as parents themselves who had lost a child that life will look different after two years. There is finally a feeling of peace and sweetness that comes to mind when I now think of Daniel. It is no longer a feeling of unbearable pain and misery. I miss him and love him with all my heart but I do know I will see him again. If I were asked knowing what I now know would I still choose to be Daniel's mother? My answer without a moment's hesitation would be absolutely yes! I would have never known so much pain and sorrow if I had not experienced so much love and joy from such a wonderful son.

November 12, 2005
"more gifts"

I was so sure that my journal was complete and a stopping off point had been reached but I must include what happened last weekend. Last Sunday night (November 6, 2005) Abby, my eight year old granddaughter was baptized. All the children had gone to Mike and Laurie's church to be a part of this very special occasion. As I sat in the row behind my children I was so thrilled to have them all in church with me. Karl was sitting next to me and I said to him, "isn't it great to have all seven children with us in church." It was a marvelous feeling. I am not sure we have all been in the same church building since Daniel's funeral.

This baptism was my first baptism for a grandchild. It means so much to me that I have a righteous daughter and son-in-law that are such good and wonderful parents. They are raising this precious child to be obedient to God's commandments and to love Heavenly Father. It was such a special evening. It was half way through the program that I was struck with this over powering feeling of Daniel's presence. At first I questioned if I were feeling the Holy Ghost which seemed to be very strong at this meeting. I quickly realized that it was most definitely Daniel's spirit I was feeling. I rested my hand on Karl's leg and looked at his face and saw that he too had tears in his eyes. I simply said to him that Daniel was here. He squeezed my hand and nodded as tears ran down his cheeks too. I knew for sure Daniel was near because Karl was feeling it too. I had not given any thought to the possibility that Daniel's spirit may be felt that night. I was very taken back by the experience. I realized that Daniel either came because this was a very important event or perhaps it was a great place to be. It made me realize that events that happen involving the family are also very important to Daniel. He is very much aware of his family. He loves us greatly and knew it was important that he be there in spirit to experience this very special occasion with his eternal family.

<u>**December 23, 2005**</u>
"semi-normal Christmas"

I feel proud of myself for being so strong and "all together" in these last few weeks. This is the first time since Daniel has died that I have felt like celebrating Christmas. For the past two years I have gone through a very pretended state of celebration. In the last two years I have managed to go through the motions of Christmas with very little feelings other than a huge feeling of sadness and loss. This year the house is decorated once again with all its splendor and finery. Gifts were bought and wrapped weeks ago. Presents tumble far out into the floor from under the tree. The house and all its beautiful decorations would look as though all is well and we are all anxiously waiting for Christmas morning. But if the truth be known it is not like the Christmases from years past. Is this Christmas better than the first Christmas he wasn't here? Yes, it is but it is also very different. The decorated house is once again a painful reminder of the Christmases that my heart longs for but is gone. In fact I heard Karl tell someone last week, "this is the first Christmas since Daniel died that we are staying home. We are trying to have a semi-normal Christmas that would resemble Christmases from the past." When I heard him say this I remember immediately thinking there is that word again, *normal.* There is nothing normal about this and it will never be a *normal* Christmas again.

I have made a very diligent effort to capture the spirit of Christmas for my self as well as for my family. There has been a great effort in more giving on my part and this does not mean material gifts. My heart has really turned to the less fortunate this year and I have loved this spirit of giving so much. But no matter how much I gave away I would never be able to give enough to fill up the empty space in my heart. There is a hole in this mother's heart that will always be there!

It is not just me because the other family members feel Daniel's void just as much as I do. A few days ago Jenny asked if I thought they celebrated Christmas in heaven and how did Daniel celebrate Christmas now? Laurie called me tonight to tell me what a rotten night she had last night because she had cried and cried. It all stemmed from her missing Daniel so much and then she thought of her parents and what that would entail to not a have a child living at Christmas time. She was feeling so sad about not having Daniel around for Christmas and yet she thought I am a mere sibling. What must a parent feel? Everyone is thinking more about him and the void of him not being here is very real. Christmas automatically makes us think about family, family time together and the love our family feels towards each other. It's not that I miss him anymore at Christmas time than

I do at any other time of year. It's because at Christmas time a spirit of love permeates the air and the love we share towards our family members is so strong.

So do I know anymore than I did my first Christmas without him? The answer is not really. Christmases are hard, no matter if it is the first year or the third. I feel as though it will be hard no matter what number year it is. I will always miss him no matter what day it is but holidays are a stark reminder that these are family days and a loved one is missing.

January 2, 2006
"be where you're supposed to be"

Another new year begins and this day has been red flagged in my mind for a long time. This day is very significant for me in regards to Jenny. I remember many months ago figuring out what day it would be when Jenny would reach the same age as Daniel was when he died. Well, today is that day. From this day forward Jenny will have lived longer than Daniel lived. I wonder if I will do the same numerical calculations in the year that Amy and Matt turn nineteen years old. Jenny was never supposed to be older than Daniel. Daniel has been frozen in my time line as the nineteen year old son who died. And yet today Jenny turns nineteen years, five months and three weeks. The exact age Daniel was when he died. It was never meant to have happened that way. Daniel is child number five and Jenny is number six. Jenny is never to be older than Daniel. I told my mom about my calculation that I had figured out. She said she had done that with her older brother. He was the oldest of the four siblings and he died at the age of twenty-six. Her other two siblings have also died and she remembers passing the age that they died and knowing she had lived longer than them. Perhaps this isn't some strange, quirky thing I am now doing with the children that are younger than Daniel. I wonder how weird it will feel to have Matt, the baby of the family, turning thirty or forty years old and still remember Daniel as the nineteen year old. Now that's a question I would like to ask a parent who has lost a child thirty or forty years ago. Is your deceased child always the age they died, no matter how many years have gone by or do you say, " if they were alive today they would have been thirty or forty something years old." I do know at the present time I always tell people I have eight children and if they ask for their ages, I say Daniel who died at age nineteen. I just wonder if this will be my answer for all the years to come.

Matt, my mom, and I were in the car today and nothing was being said about Daniel at the time. Out of the blue Matt asks what I would do if I were to wake up and realize this was all a dream. What if I woke up on the Sunday morning he died and this had all been a dream? I told him the first thing I would do is go to his room and make sure he was still there and it was indeed all a dream. Then I would be the happiest mom in the world. Matt added a very interesting comment, he said, "I bet you would have made sure he went to church so he wouldn't have stayed home. That way he wouldn't have been home to answer the telephone from her." I think I know why Matt has come up with this idea. We have been talking to him about being where you are supposed to be. If he has scouts or a scout outing then that's where he is suppose to be. It's less likely you are going to get into trouble if you are where you are suppose to be.

March 4, 2006

I have now passed the third year anniversary. The anniversary of the death date is always a strange day. Even after three years I still don't know what to do with that day. Weeks ahead of time you know its coming. There is a sense of dread and yet I am not sure what I'm dreading. Some days it feels as though my mind is telling me, "get ready, March 2nd is fast approaching." I feel myself getting geared up for something that I have no control over. I have no idea what I am getting geared up for or what I should be preparing myself for. I now have three years of this same experience and each year proves to be as the year before. I live with this dreaded fear of the calendar turning to March 2nd and once again my fear of the day is always worst than the actual anniversary. I continue to wake up on March 2nd and miss him just as much as I did the day before, the week before even the year before. The anniversary date has nothing to do with me missing him more or grieving more. I know that I will never look at March 2nd as just another day but I am learning that this date need not carry so much fear and dread for me. I have no intentions of ever honoring this date or bringing attention to the fact that Daniel died on this date. I do know that every March 2nd that I live will be a day that I will never forget. In my mind I will always reflect on this day as the day that changed my life forever. It was the day I began *searching for my new normal.*

I knew from the very first anniversary that I would not use his death date as a day to hold any type of celebration. The first anniversary of his death was a special day because it was a day of deep reflection. It was an evening that consisted of beautiful memories and stories that were shared by his family and friends. I took from that evening a very important lesson. Daniel was so much more than the Sunday afternoon he died. Daniel was all about the nineteen wonderful years that he lived. I knew then that I would not choose to give any kind of formal recognition for the following anniversaries of his death date. Daniel was truly about living.

There will never be closure when a parent loses a child. In this journey called grief I have learned that healing is an on going process. I have learned so much about myself because of this experience. I have no idea why I was dealt this experience but I do know that we all learn and grow from life's experiences. I have chosen not to stay frozen in the debilitating stage of grief and sadness. I will not punish myself and my family because of Daniel's death. I will choose to honor Daniel and Daniel's life. As stated earlier, Daniel was so much more than the day he died. I must not ever lose sight of that statement and the power it holds for me. I know my son and I know Daniel would never want his mother to live a life with so much pain and misery. I will honor Daniel and honor Daniel's life by the way I now choose to live. With all that I now know and all that I have suffered, I would choose without a moment's hesitation to still be Daniel's mother. There would have never been so much pain and unbelievable heartache if there had not been so much love. My love for Daniel is eternal.

I am beginning to see my "new normal" on the horizon and it doesn't look so strange or bad after all. I know it is there and that's what keeps me going. I have learned to accept the fact that it won't look like the life I had before Daniel died and that's ok. It has taken a very long journey to finally admit that I am going to be ok and my family is going to make it too.

March 14, 2006

At the time of this writing it has been over three years since Daniel died. I wish I could write and tell you that all is well and my grieving is now complete. It is not, but what I can tell you and what you must hold onto is, it does get better. All my life I have heard that time heals. Before Daniel's death I wasn't so sure I believed it and I certainly doubt those words today. I know I am not healed but I am healing. I am so much better physically, and emotionally than I was the day I wrote the first entry in this journal. I still have unanswered questions and I do know that I will live the rest of my life not knowing the answers for many of those questions. I have also come to realize that even if Daniel was to stand right before me this day and tell me why, I would have trouble accepting it and I certainly would not like it. So spending the enormous amount of energy that it would take to continue to search for answers would all be for naught. I would never accept or understand his answer.

There is one other certainty and that is I know I will never get completely over this. I am *searching for my new normal*. The life that I knew before March 2, 2003 is over and will never exist again. There is a great line in a movie that rings so true. It says that life can change in a matter of seconds and then you are left with the "before" and the "after". I have learned that I will not fully recover but I have learned that I have coping skills and inner powers of strength that I never knew existed. I have also discovered the most amazing love, kindness and compassion of friends and family that has made my journey in the last three years even remotely possible. I was never restricted by boundaries of distance or time on a clock because they have always been there for me. My recommendation for anyone going through grief is to reach out more. In hindsight I wished I had done more reaching out to loved ones and less solitaire mourning. They are there for you but have no idea what to say or do. Sometimes just knowing they were there if ever I needed them was enough to keep me going. So much of my early grieving and mourning was done alone because I could not have imagined being in any one's presence during such debilitating circumstances. Even though I know they would have not been able to comprehend my loss completely unless they too had lost a child, I do know they love me and would never be judgmental. A soft shoulder to cry on instead of a bed pillow would have been nicer.

My absolute greatest thanks would be to my Father in Heaven. I would have never begun to have made it thus far without His love and comfort. He has never once left me comfortless. I never questioned if He was with me. I have always known He was right beside me. It has taken the most tragic and horrible event in my life to bring forth the most spiritual experiences of my life. Even today three years later I still grieve and cry for Daniel. I cry and mourn for his loss because I miss him so much. I do not doubt where he is and how he is doing. I have always known that I will see Daniel again and we will be reunited as a family. My heart aches for the mothers who do not have this sure knowledge for themselves concerning their own children. It is this sure knowledge that helps me get up every morning, otherwise I know I would stay in bed with the covers over my head all day, everyday. I miss Daniel terribly and long for the day to be back in his presence but I know that I will see Daniel again. I have never questioned if I will see Daniel again. That is one question I have never had-Thank you God.

Afterword

By Karl C. Williams

I was very pleased when Rexanne asked me to write an afterword to give an update on the family. In addition to an update on our family I would like to share my thoughts about her journal and then add a few of my own personal feelings.

My first impression of her book is that it is different. Most of the books on this subject that I have read are very clinical, written by professionals trying to describe grief, or written by someone who is attempting to recall the past. Rexanne's book is an actual journal. It allows you to see the real grief and sorrow as it unfolds.

Rexanne expressed some very personal and emotional experiences in her journal that she had never intended for anyone to read. Because of this she has been very reluctant to publish it for the world to see. She has expressed the fear of strangers criticizing her writing or maybe worse being critical of her, not understanding what she has gone through. I truly think the only people who have a clue are those that have lost children themselves.

As you read her journal you will find that the good days and bad days have entries while the "just coping days" are left without any comment. It was often that we would go through a day looking ok on the outside. We would hear comments like; "you look like you are handling this so well." In reality we were dying inside with very little brain function. It was just enough to go through the motions of a "normal" day. I think the mere fact that her journal entries get further and further apart as time goes on is an indication of healing.

Now for an update on the children: Everyone still comes over on the first Sunday of each month for dinner at Grammy's and Papa's house. We now have eight grandchildren with two more on the way. Laurie is thirty-two; she and Mike are still living in the area with their three children. Joseph, our oldest son is thirty and has graduated from the University of Florida and also lives in the area. Melissa is twenty-nine; she and Tim have three children with one on the way and they also live in the area. Michael who is twenty-seven years old has married Bridget and they have two children and live in the area. Jennifer is married to David and is expecting their first child. Amy who is nineteen years old has graduated from high school and attends college. Matthew is sixteen years old and attends high school. Penny the golden retriever has since passed away and is with Daniel.

From the very beginning we have never tried to hide the fact that Daniel took his own life. We have never been embarrassed about it, just completely shocked. I remember some friends telling me very early on how brave we were to be so honest about it. It was the right decision. This has helped in the healing process of not worrying about hiding something that didn't need to be hidden.

Months after Daniel's death I decided to put his car back together. I wanted to drive that car again. This was going to be an enormous task. There were two motors in the garage with all their parts and bolts spread about and moved around now for months. I had not been involved in taking his car apart. It had been decades since I worked on a car other than the occasional assistance with Daniel's car. How do I start, where do I start, and which parts are extra parts for the other motor were my questions as I began this monumental task? There were screws, nuts and bolts everywhere. The experience of repairing Daniel's car was amazing. Throughout the entire process I felt guided by the spirit and I also felt that Daniel was nearby. The car is still running today.

A sweet soul gave us a tree shortly after Daniel's death and we planted it in the front yard. We all call it the Daniel tree. It wasn't until recently that Rexanne and I discovered we share the same fear. The fear is each year when all the leaves fall we wonder if it will come back next year. I think this shows us that we will never get over this tragedy because Daniel's death is always in the back of our mind.

After this experience and the number of times that I have been comforted, not by man but by the spirit, I have a new favorite scripture. It is found in John 14:18 "I will not leave you comfortless: I will come to you."

Life will always have its ups and downs, but no matter how hard it gets there will always be an up after the down which will bring joy to your life. So the bottom line: Life is worth living!

For more information about our family, Daniel or the book, go to www.searchingforthenewnormal.com.

APPENDIX

The appendix's purpose is to explain the references to our church that are used through out the journal entries. It is also a place for the songs and poems that helped along the way.

The Church of Jesus Christ of Latter-day Saints

-Bishop: A man who has been ordained and set apart as the presiding High Priest for a ward. He has responsibility for the temporal and spiritual wellbeing of all his ward members.

-Comforter: The Holy Ghost.

-First Presidency: A quorum of three men that presides over the entire Church; made up of the President of the Church and his Counselors.

-General Authority: These brethren are all delegated general administrative authority by the President of the Church. That is, they are called to preach the Gospel, direct Church Conferences and handle the properties of the Church generally. The labors of their ministries are not confined to a stake, ward, or regional areas, but they have general jurisdiction in all parts of the Church.

-General Conference: A semi-annual conference which is held for the entire membership of the Church and is broadcast worldwide.

-Patriarchal Blessing: An inspired blessing given by a patriarch, declaring a persons linage and giving inspired counsel and insight about his or her life.

-Relief Society: A Church organization of adult women whose purpose is to work for the temporal and spiritual salvation of all the women of the Church.

-Stake: Made up of several Wards.

-Stake President: Presides over a stake and is responsible for and directs all the programs of the Church within his stake area.

-Temple: A place of worship and prayer; the house of the Lord prepared and dedicated for sacred gospel ordnances.

-Temple recommend: Required for entrance into a dedicated Latter-day Saint temple, it is only available to members who pass worthiness interviews by their local church leaders.

-Ward: The basic Church unit in and through which the programs of the Church are administered. Members of a ward form a congregation who worship under the direction of a Bishop.

Scriptural references cited in the journal on 2 June 2003:

Book of Mormon, Alma 7: 11-12 "And he shall go forth, suffering pains and afflictions and temptations of every kind; and this that the word might be fulfilled which saith he will take upon him the pains and sicknesses of his people. And he will take upon him death, that he may lose the bands of death which bind his people; and he will take upon him their infirmities, that his bowels may be filled with mercy, according to the flesh, that he may know according to the flesh how to succor his people according to their infirmities."

Doctrine and Covenants 138: 58-59 "The dead who repent will be redeemed, through obedience to the ordnances of the house of God. And after they have paid the penalty of their transgressions, and are washed clean, shall receive a reward according to their works, for they are heirs of salvation."

For more information about the Church of Jesus Christ of Latter-day Saints see www.lds.org.

About the Author

Rexanne Williams, the mother of eight children, resides in Virginia Beach, Virginia. She has been married thirty-three years to her sweetheart, Karl. She enjoys teaching early morning seminary for the youth of her church. She has had the opportunity to live in various states on the East and gulf coast of America. She may be contacted via **www.searchingforthenewnormal.com**.

978-0-595-45242-2
0-595-45242-6

Printed in the United States
201077BV00004B/274-297/P